Eat Your Way Around the World

by Jamie Aramini

Cover Design
Alex Wiggers

Eat Your Way Around the World
by Jamie Aramini

Published by Geography Matters®

ISBN 978-1-931397-36-0
Library of Congress Control Number: 2007925217
Printed in the United States of America

Dedication

To my husband, Joe,
for your willingness to eat even the most exotic foods
without complaining—I love you.

About the Author

Jamie Aramini is the author of *Geography Through Art* with Sharon Jeffus and *The Adventures of Munford* series. Jamie graduated co-valedictorian of her high school class and was a Kentucky Governor's Scholar. Now she is a stay-at-home wife and mother whose interests include organic gardening, cooking, and making stuffed animals from old socks. Jamie can't wait to start homeschooling her one-year-old son, but in the mean time entertains herself by teaching a writing class to the very creative students at the local homeschool co-op. Visit Jamie's website at www.jamiearamini.com.

Table of Contents

Introduction

Asia

Europe

South America

Oceania

Appendix

Art projects for these countries can be found in *Geography Through Art* by Sharon Jeffus and Jamie Aramini.

Introduction

How To Use This Book

Eat Your Way Around the World can be used in several ways. You can take your family on a whirlwind tour of the world, eating a meal from a different country each week of the month. Alternately, you could use the meals in this book to introduce each country as you study it. This should really help spark the imaginations of all the children in your home. How great it would be to have an English tea party before studying about Parliament!

One of my favorite ways to use this book is to use it at the end of the study of a particular country. Invite friends and family and treat them to an international meal. Have your kids tell what they have learned about the country. Be creative! Don't just limit them to reading a country report. Perhaps they could sing a song in the native tongue or read a popular children's story for that area.

A great way to learn about the culture of a country is to learn about the country's art. What better way to learn than to make the art yourself? Use my book, *Geography Through Art* with Sharon Jeffus, to find fun art projects from countries all over the world. Countries with corresponding projects are marked with this symbol throughout the cookbook and in the Table of Contents.

The Recipes

When researching this book, I tried to choose recipes that were historically the most popular for a country. As technology advances and the world becomes more and more connected, the culture of each country slowly meshes with the countries near it and even the countries on the other side of the world. This especially is apparent in a nation's cuisine. While at one time the food of England may have just been that—English food—now it is a mix of food that visitors and immigrants have imported from all over the world. I have tried my best to focus on what is traditionally eaten in a country, rather than giving a foreign recipe just because the English love Indian food or the Americans love Chinese!

I adapted recipes to be as simple as possible and to use ingredients widely available no matter what country you are in. You should be able to find the ingredients in any grocery store. No special trips to an ethnic or specialty food store needed! Each recipe is rated for ease of preparation. The simplest recipes are one fork, and the most complicated are four forks.

Make More Than Dinner!

The more authentic the dining experience is, the more your kids will love it! Try the following suggestions and use the space provided with each country to jot down ideas for making it more than dinner:

- **Set the table.** Try to set the table with decorations and colors from that country. Visit your local fabric store for fabrics that might work. You can also visit an import store for affordable decorations from the country of your choice. Check out books from your local library that contain pictures of what life is like. Some other decoration ideas might include flags or maps of the country.

- **Set the tone.** One of the best ways to set the mood is to play music from the country you are studying. Visit your local library to see their selection of world music. If they don't have what you are looking for, talk to the librarian to see if they can request it through the InterLibrary Loan program. You can also look online at worldmusic.nationalgeographic.com and www.smithsonianglobalsound.org.

- **Learn the Language.** Learn a few words in the native language of the country you are studying. Say What! sections throughout the book will give you a jump start. See how many words you can use through the course of the meal.

- **Dress the part.** Research the native dress from the country. Make costumes for the whole family. These do not have to be elaborate. It could be as simple as a sheet wrapped like an Indian sari or a sombrero for Latin America.

- **Do the research.** Try to find someone in your community who has lived in or spent extensive time in the country. Most people would be more than happy to tell you about their experiences. Be sure to invite them to your dinner as a thank you for all their help!

Food Activities

- **Be a food critic.** Have each child record their response to the meal. Sweet? Salty? Bitter? Creamy? Chunky? Rich? Descriptive adjectives are a must! A thesaurus would be helpful. This is a great way to expand their vocabulary. Some samples from a newspaper or magazine might help get the creative juices flowing. It is also helpful to compare new dishes with familiar tastes and textures.

- **Be a travel agent.** Have your child create a brochure or poster advertising the country's culture. Be sure to highlight the local cuisine! If you are inviting guests, make these ahead of time and use as invitations.

- **Be a travel journalist.** After each meal is over (and the dishes are done!), have your child record his thoughts about his "trip" to the country. What sights did he see and sounds did he hear? Be sure to include photos or even drawings!

- **Fill a passport.** This is a great way to help picky eaters expand their horizons. Designate a small notebook as the child's "passport." For each country they "visit," let them add a stamp for the country. (Tasting all the foods is a requirement!) Use stamps you already have on hand, or let the kids draw their own. Check out the passport in the Appendix created just for this purpose. Copy the passport or cut out of the book. If you copy the stamps on adhesive paper you've created stamp stickers.

- **Have a world travel night!** This is a great group project, perfect for school classrooms or homeschool co-ops. Have each child prepare a dish from a different country along with a creative poster telling important facts. (This would be a quick way to fill up the passports!) Although the recipes serve four to six people, they could easily be multiplied to serve more.

- **Keep a food journal.** A food journal is a great way to keep track of your favorite meals and to remember your food experiences. You can start one by making copies of the sample page in the back of the book. Just fill in the blanks after each meal and you are ready to go! Keep the pages in a folder or three-ring binder. You don't have to limit your food journal to meals from this book. You can use it to record any memorable meal event!

Bon appétit,

Jamie Aramini

(Please note: I would be happy to hear your feedback about the book. Any questions, comments, or suggestions would be appreciated. If you prepare a special ethnic meal using this book, please let me know about it! I would love to hear all the details! Email me at jamiearamini@yahoo.com.)

Africa

Egypt is often called "The Gift of the Nile." Farmers have harnessed the power of the Nile to create fertile cropland with abundant results for millenniums. In fact, a large amount of the world's food knowledge from ancient times has come from Egyptian walls, art, and pyramids.

Gebna Makleyah

These cheese balls are a delicious appetizer and the kids will love getting their hands messy to make them!

1 cup crumbled feta cheese
1 T flour
1 egg
3 T olive oil
salt and pepper

1. Preheat oven to 400°F. Mix cheese, flour, and egg well in a bowl. This is easiest if you use your hands—as long as you wash them first! Salt and pepper to taste.
2. Roll mixture into walnut sized balls. If the mixture falls apart, add more flour. If the mixture is too dry, add a little water.
3. Cover a cookie sheet with the olive oil. Roll the balls on the cookie sheet to coat with oil.

4. Bake for ten minutes, shaking the cookie sheet (with an oven mitt, of course) every two or three minutes to turn the balls and prevent burning. Serve when lightly golden.

Biram Ruz

This rice casserole, an Egyptian classic, is an excellent accompaniment to almost any dish from Africa!

2 cups long grain rice
2 cups whole milk
2 cups heavy cream
½ tsp salt
½ tsp pepper
1 T butter

1. Preheat oven to 400°F. Combine milk and cream in a saucepan; bring to a light boil. (Be careful not to burn it!)
2. In a casserole dish, add rice, cream mixture, salt, and pepper. Bake, covered, for thirty five minutes.
3. Uncover and slice butter into rice. Cook uncovered for twenty minutes more or until rice is browned on top.

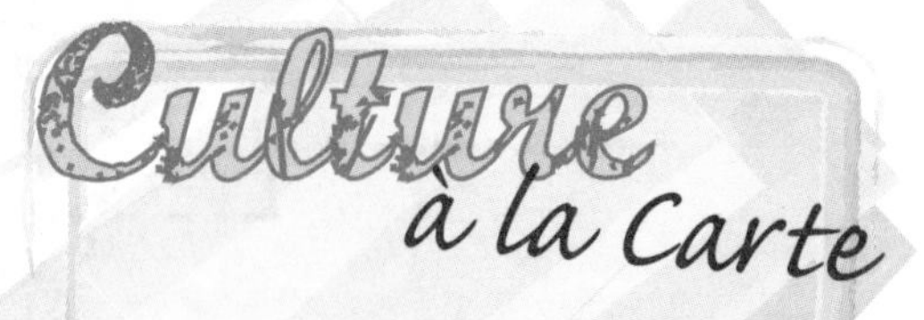

- In Ancient Egypt, taxes were often paid with honey.
- The first recorded watermelon harvest took place in Egypt.
- Wealthy Egyptians of the past ate off of plates made of silver, gold, or bronze.

Food Profile: The Onion

The onion was highly valued by the ancient Egyptians — they believed that the many layers represented eternity. They even placed their hands on an onion to take an oath! Traces of onion have been found in the tombs of many pharaohs and other ancient Egyptians.

Have you ever wandered why cutting an onion makes you cry? It is because the gases released by the onion's cells when it is cut irritate your eyes. If you want to avoid these troublesome tears, the best way is to wear goggles to protect your eyes from the gases. If this seems a little nerdy, try chilling the onion in the fridge beforehand, which helps neutralize the gases, or cut it under running water.

Shish Kebabs

1 lb ribeye, cubed
1 T cumin
1 tsp salt
1 tsp ground ginger
½ tsp cinnamon
⅛ tsp ground cloves
2 garlic cloves, minced
2 large onions, cut in wedges
2 T olive oil

1. Combine all ingredients but onion in a plastic container. Cover and marinate for thirty minutes in refrigerator.
2. Preheat oven to 400°F. Thread meat and onions onto skewers.
3. Bake for twenty-five minutes or until meat is done. (Alternately, these can be grilled.)

Make More Than Dinner!

Ethiopia is in northern Africa, between the countries of Sudan and Somalia. The mountainous terrain has traditionally prevented Ethiopia from having much interaction with the outside world, thus leaving the native food culture largely intact. The cuisine of Ethiopia is famous because of its extreme spiciness—so hot that many foreigners cannot eat it—and because the meal is served without utensils or plates!

Dine Ethiopian-style!

A traditional Ethiopian meal begins with a pitcher of water and an empty basin. Water is poured from the pitcher over the right hand of each guest, the excess water going into the basin. The hands are then dried on a hand towel. The left hand is not used during dining. This may prove quite difficult, especially if you are left-handed! After the handwashing, the *injera,* a large flatbread, is placed directly on the table, covering it much like a tablecloth. The *injera* we will prepare probably won't be big enough to cover the whole table, so you can just place a large piece in front of each person. (If placing it directly on the table makes you uncomfortable, place some aluminum foil underneath.) The food is then served directly on the *injera.* To eat, tear off a piece of the *injera* (right hand only!), and scoop up the food. Dessert is not traditionally served in Ethiopia, although small cups of coffee are brought out after the meal.

Make your own Berbere!

This is a spice mix, red in color, used as a base for many Ethiopian dishes. You may be able to purchase it at an ethnic food store, or you can make this simple version at home. Simply mix the ingredients in a baking dish, then bake in a 300 degree oven for twenty minutes. Be sure to stir frequently to keep from burning! When you are done, store in an airtight container.

1/8 tsp cinnamon
1/8 tsp allspice
1/8 tsp cloves
1/4 tsp coriander
1/4 tsp cardamom
1/4 tsp nutmeg
1/2 tsp black pepper
1/2 tsp ginger
1 T salt
1/4 cup paprika
1/2 cup cayenne pepper

Yataklete Kilkil (Ginger Vegetables)

3 cups water
3 potatoes, peeled and sliced
2 carrots, sliced
¼ lb. fresh green beans, trimmed
3 T vegetable oil
1 onion, chopped
1 green bell pepper, seeded and sliced
1 jalapeno pepper, seeded and sliced
1 garlic clove, peeled and chopped
1 1-inch piece fresh ginger, peeled and chopped
1 tsp salt
½ tsp pepper
3 green onions, chopped

1. Bring water to a boil. Add potatoes, carrots, and green beans. Return to a boil. Continue boiling for five minutes. Remove from heat; drain.
2. In a large skillet, saute onion, green pepper, jalapeno, garlic, and ginger in vegetable oil until they begin to soften. Add potato mixture to skillet along with salt, pepper, and green onions. Stir well.
3. Continue cooking until vegetables reach desired level of doneness. They are best if they retain some crispness.

Injera

If you are not able to make the *injera,* use pita bread or flour tortillas as a substitute.

3½ cups warm water, divided
1 package (¼ oz) active dry yeast
1 tsp sugar
3 cups flour
¼ cup whole wheat flour
½ cup cornmeal
1 T baking powder
1 T salt
1½ cups water, divided

1. Combine ¼ cup of the warm water with the yeast and sugar. Let sit until foamy, about ten minutes. Add remaining ingredients except last 1 1/2 cup water and stir well. Cover with a damp cloth and let rise until doubled, about one hour.
2. Punch down dough. Mix in a blender, two cups at a time. Add ½ cup water with each batch. The mixture will be liquid.
3. Heat a large skillet to medium-low heat. Pour a thin layer of batter in the skillet. (No need to add anything to the bottom to prevent sticking.) When bubbles form over the entire surface, the *injera* is done. You do not need to flip it to cook the other side. Remove with a spatula, and place right on the table! Your Ethiopian plate is ready!

Doro Wot (Chicken Stew)

This stew is not for the faint of stomach! To make it less spicy, cut back on the amount of *berbere.*

2 T butter
2 red onions, chopped
4 garlic cloves, chopped
2 tsp salt
½ tsp ground cumin
½ tsp ground cardamom
½ tsp ground nutmeg
2 T berbere (p. 8)
1 1-inch piece fresh ginger, peeled and chopped
2 lb. boneless chicken thighs, cubed
1 lemon, juiced
1 cup chicken stock
4 eggs, hard-boiled with shells removed

1. In a medium pot, saute onion and garlic in butter until onions are tender. Add salt, cumin, cardamom, nutmeg, berbere, and ginger. Stir well.
2. Add in lemon juice and chicken stock. Bring to a boil. Stir in chicken. Reduce heat, cover, and simmer for twenty minutes
3. Pierce eggs with a fork and add to stew. Turn chicken to be sure it is coated with sauce. Continue simmering until chicken is done, another fifteen or twenty minutes. Serve warm, draining off excess juice before placing on *injera.* Each person receives one of the eggs.

Culture à la Carte

- Each Ethiopian woman has her own mix of berbere. Many believe that the tastier the mix, the better off she will be when finding a husband.
- For many years, bars of salt were used as currency in Ethiopia.
- The coffee bean was originally discovered in Ethiopia.

Make More Than Dinner!

The nation of Kenya is famous for the spectacular variety of wildlife it contains, everything from lions and giraffes to zebras and elephants. Kenya has a booming tourist industry with visitors from all over the world coming to see these animals. Most native Kenyans, however, live a simple life and often struggle to feed their families. Many meals in Kenya are made to provide the most amount of sustenance for the smallest amount of money. Meat, for example, is a luxury that not all Kenyans can afford.

Irio

1 cup canned peas
1 cup canned corn
5 medium potatoes, peeled and cubed
1 cup canned spinach
water
2 T butter
salt
pepper

1. Combine peas, corn, potatoes, and spinach in a pot. Cover with water; bring to a boil.
2. Boil until tender, about fifteen minutes. Drain.
3. Add butter; salt and pepper to taste. Mash.

Say What!

Try talking in Swahili, one of the national languages of Kenya, while you eat your meal!

eat: kula
drink: kunywa
food: chakula
bowl: bakuli
plate: sahani
spoon: kijiko
salt: chumui
pepper: piripiri
please: tafadhali
thank you: asante
sorry: samahani
yes: ndio
no: hapana

Sukuma Wiki

Sukuma wiki translated means "stretch the week." It is commonly served towards the end of the week in Kenya with leftover meat and whatever veggies haven't been used up already. If you would like to add meat, try cooked ground beef.

$2\frac{1}{4}$ cups water, divided
1 lb greens (kale, collard, and/or spinach)
2 T flour
1 lemon, juiced
2 T vegetable oil
1 onion, chopped
1 tomato, chopped
1 green chili, seeded and chopped
salt

1. Bring two cups of water to a boil; add greens. Cover and cook until nearly tender; drain.
2. In a small bowl, stir flour, lemon juice, and remaining water until smooth.
3. Heat oil in a separate skillet. Saute onion, tomatoes, and chili together. Salt to taste.
4. Add flour mixture and stir until smooth. Reduce heat and add greens; cover and simmer over low heat until greens are tender and sauce is thickened.

- Coconut milk, called madafu, is a popular Kenyan drink.
- Fish is a common meal for school-age children because it is believed to make one more intelligent.
- Sour milk, called maziwa mala, is eaten all over Kenya. It is often used as a topping for ugali.

Ugali

This side dish is eaten with nearly every meal in Kenya!

1 cup milk
1¼ cups cornmeal, divided
1 cup water, boiling

1. Whisk milk and ¾ cup of the cornmeal until it becomes a paste. Stir into boiling water; reduce heat to low. Slowly add the remaining ½ cup of cornmeal, stirring constantly. The mixture should be smooth with no lumps.
2. Cook for about three minutes. When the mixture begins to stick together and pull away from the sides of the pan, remove from heat. Pour into a greased serving bowl and allow to cool.

Make More Than Dinner!

Locate Morocco on a world map, and you'll see why its cuisine is influenced by many cultures. The Strait of Gilbraltar separates the country from Spain by only a few miles, and its shipping ports have opened Moroccan kitchens up to influence from all over the Mediterranean and the world. Moroccans are famous for their elaborate feasts, called *diffas.* A typical *diffa* lasts for hours and could have as many as fifty courses! We will prepare a miniature *diffa* for your dining pleasure.

Have A Moroccan Feast!

Meals in Morocco are typically eaten at a low table with everyone sitting on cushions. You might try sitting at a coffee table. When decorating the table, remember that Morocco is famous for rich, vibrant colors—deep red, terra cotta, royal blue, and aquamarine. Gold or copper is a common accent color. Meals are often eaten outside, surrounded by palm trees, so be sure to bring any houseplants to the dining room. Each dish is served as a separate course. (I've listed the recipes in the order they should be served.) Large portions are a sign of hospitality—very rarely could you clean your plate at a Moroccan meal!

Lamb Chops

4 lamb chops
2 T olive oil
2 tsp cumin
2 tsp coriander
1½ tsp salt
¼ tsp cinnamon
¼ tsp red pepper flakes
2 cloves garlic, minced

1. Mix together all ingredients except lamb in a bowl. Marinate in refrigerator for half an hour.
2. Preheat skillet to medium; add lamb chops and marinade. Cook until meat is done, about five minutes per side.

Tangine (Stew)

To make this dish a meal of its own, add cubed beef or lamb. Serve with *couscous*, steamed semolina grains available at your local supermarket in the rice section. In Morocco, the *couscous* is served on a large platter in the middle of the table. Everyone uses their right hand, takes a handful, rolls it into a ball, and eats it with a bite of the *tangine.* If you are adventurous enough to try this serving method, be sure that everyone washes their hands first!

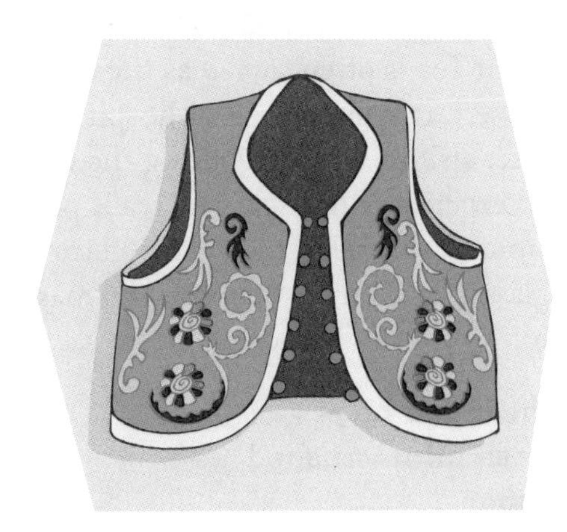

4 cups water
4 potatoes, peeled and sliced
3 carrots, peeled and chopped
3 celery stalks, chopped
2 turnips, peeled and chopped
4 zucchini, chopped
2 T olive oil
1 small red chili, chopped
1 tsp cumin
2 T fresh parsley
1 onion, peeled and chopped

1. Bring water to a boil in a large stock pot. Add all vegetables except the zucchini, chili, and the onion. Cook for ten minutes.
2. While vegetable are cooking, heat the olive oil in a small pan. Add chili, cumin, parsley, and onion; saute for five minutes. After vegetables have cooked for ten minutes, add the zucchini and the onion mix.
3. Cook until the liquid is reduced and vegetables are tender, about ten minutes.

Food Profile: Couscous

Couscous, a favorite Moroccan food, is made from steamed durum wheat grains. You will find it in the rice section at the grocery store. This couscous is presteamed for easy preparation, but in Morocco the grains would have to be steamed three or four times before eating. Because of this, several families will sometimes get together and steam a huge portion of couscous together, so that the workload can be shared. Couscous is served with most meals in Morocco—sometimes even as a dessert!

Shay bil na'na' (Mint Tea)

Mint Tea is often served as the only dessert. It is also a sign of hospitality to offer visitors a glass. Pouring the tea is an experience in itself. The tea is poured from a great height into very narrow glasses. It is an art that must be mastered by every Moroccan hostess.

green tea bags
fresh mint, crushed
sugar

1. Prepare green tea according to package directions, adding the mint while the tea steeps.
2. Strain tea; add sugar to taste. Serve in narrow heatproof glasses, garnished with a sprig of mint.

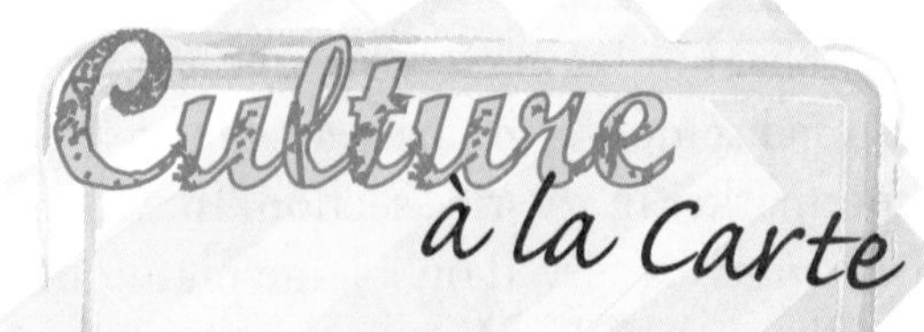

- Soup is commonly eaten for breakfast in Morocco.
- Lunch is the main meal of the day.
- When visiting a Moroccan home, it is important to bring a gift for the hostess of pastries, nuts, fruits, or flowers.

Make More Than Dinner!

Nigerians generally do not rely on recipes. Cooking traditions are passed from mother to daughter, and rarely written down. "A pinch of this, a dash of that, cooked until done," would be a usual recipe. This oral tradition causes great variations in Nigerian cuisine from region to region and family to family.

Dine Nigerian Style

Nigerian meals are usually filled with relatives—aunts, uncles, cousins. The women share the duties of preparing the food, and everyone eats the large meals together. Nigerians eat sitting on the floor. Only the very wealthy use utensils to eat; the common person uses the right hand only. (Nigeria is mainly populated by Muslims, who believe that the left hand is unclean.) It is believed that using a fork or knife would ruin the flavor and the enjoyment one gets from eating food. The elders dine first, always leaving a little on their plate for the children to eat when they are finished.

Dodo (Fried Plantains)

2 ripe plantains, peeled
2 eggs
2 tsp salt
peanut oil

1. Cover the bottom layer of a large frying pan with peanut oil; heat to medium.
2. Whisk egg and salt in a bowl. Cut the plantains in half, then slice lengthwise and dip in egg mixture. Fry in oil until lightly browned on both sides.
3. Drain on paper towels; serve.

Jollof Rice

In Nigeria, this would most likely be served with grilled goat. You can serve it plain with the Groundnut Stew (p. 19), or add strips of grilled beef or chicken.

1 onion, chopped
2 T vegetable oil
2 tsp tomato paste
1 cup long grain rice, cooked
1 green chili, seeded and chopped
1 cup beef broth

1. Saute onion in vegetable oil until soft. Add tomato paste and chili; stir on medium heat for two minutes.
2. Add rice; stir. Add broth and bring to a boil. Reduce heat to medium and cook until the broth has evaporated.

- When a woman gets married, her mother gives her a wooden spoon as a gift and a reminder that good cooking will keep a marriage strong.
- In some tribes, it is believed that a small amount of honey and salt placed on the tongue of a new baby will give it a long life.
- The Yoruba tribe measures wealth on how many yams a man owns.

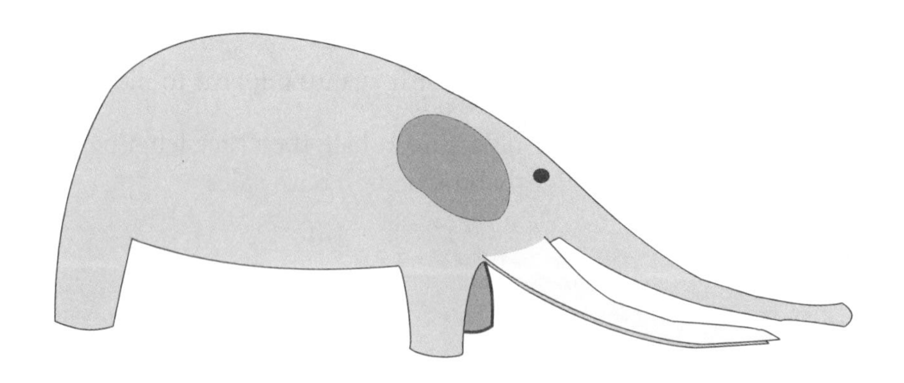

Groundnut Stew

In Nigeria, a peanut is called a "groundnut." Try this flavorful stew made with "groundnut" butter!

3 T vegetable oil
1½ lbs beef stew meat
1 onion, chopped
1 green pepper, seeded and chopped
1 (28 oz) can diced tomatoes
1 tsp salt
1 tsp red pepper flakes
¾ cups unsalted, unsweetened peanut butter
½ cup beef broth

1. Heat vegetable oil in a medium stockpot. Add beef, onion, and green pepper. Cook until beef is browned and onions are soft. Strain through a colander to remove excess fat, then add tomatoes (with juice), salt, and red pepper flakes. Bring to a boil.

2. Reduce heat; cover and simmer for forty minutes.
3. Melt peanut butter with beef broth over low heat; add to stew. Return to a boil, then reduce heat. Simmer for twenty more minutes. Skim off fat and serve.

Make More Than Dinner!

South Africa is called the "Rainbow Nation" because of the diversity of people living within its borders. The population includes descendants of the native African people, of 17th century Dutch settlers, of Indonesian slaves brought in by the Dutch settlers, and, lastly, French Huguenot refugees from around the same time period. All these varieties of cultures have combined to make a cuisine filled with delicious variety.

Sweet Potato Fritters

3 sweet potatoes, peeled and cubed
3 eggs
1 T flour
2 T butter
salt to taste
milk
breadcrumbs
vegetable oil

1. Boil potatoes until tender; mash.
2. Beat one of the eggs; stir into sweet potatoes along with flour, butter, and salt. The mixture should feel like a soft dough. If it doesn't, thicken by adding more flour or thin by adding a little milk.
3. Shape mixture into several round, flat cakes. Beat remaining eggs. Dip cakes into egg, then coat with breadcrumbs.
4. Fry in hot oil until golden brown. Drain on paper towels; serve.

Food Profile: Sweet Potatoes

Sweet potatoes are not a member of the same plant family as a regular potato. They are actually a member of the morning glory family. Sweet potatoes are not just used for dinner — other uses include animal feed, fabric dye, and some medicinal purposes. Select sweet potatoes that are firm with few nicks or bruises. Storing sweet potatoes in the refrigerator will cause them to ruin. Instead, they should be stored in a cool, dry place with no sunlight.

Bobotie

2 T butter
1 small onion, chopped
1 apple, peeled and diced
1½ lbs ground beef, cooked
2 bread slices, soaked in milk
½ T curry powder
1 T slivered almonds
1 egg
1 T lemon juice
¼ tsp turmeric
3 bay leaves
¼ cup milk
2 eggs

1. Preheat oven to 325°F. Saute onions in butter until soft. Add apple; saute a minute more. Stir in beef.
2. Tear up bread; add to beef mixture along with curry powder, almonds, lemon juice, one egg and turmeric. Stir. Place in a greased baking dish, bay leaves on top.
3. Bake, covered, for twenty-five minutes. Whisk together remaining egg and milk, then pour over beef. Bake for fifteen minutes more.
4. Discard bay leaves; serve.

Mealie Bread

2 cups biscuit mix
1 cup creamed corn
1 T sugar
1 egg
½ cup milk
¼ cup butter, melted

1. Preheat oven to 350°F.
2. Combine all ingredients except butter; stir. Place in a greased 9-inch baking pan. Coat with melted butter.
3. Bake for twenty minutes; serve.

- The Bantu tribe's prized food is emasi, milk that has been soured in a gourd. Each person is only permitted to eat emasi from his own tribe. Even a women who marries into another tribe can only eat emasi from her new tribe after the birth of her first child.
- A plump wife is a sign of wealth among the Bantu people. A man with a plump wife will attract more wives to his household.
- South Africans have traditionally used hollowed termite hills as a kind of oven to bake bread.

Make More Than Dinner!

Asia

The country of China contains nearly twenty percent of the world's population. Chinese cuisine is popular all over the world! It may be one of the international cuisines with which you are the most familiar. In fact, you may have already sampled the food at your local Chinese restaurant.

How To Serve A Chinese Meal

Chinese culture places great importance on the value of family and the elderly to society. Hence, the best food is always served first to the eldest person at the table. No one starts eating until this person does, and no one else gets up from the table until they do.

Chinese meals usually take place at round tables with the guest of honor (once again, usually the oldest person) facing the door. Each person at the table should be served their own bowl of plain white rice. (Simply purchase and prepare according to package directions.) Hot tea is generally served with each meal, as cold drinks are believed to hinder digestion. A final cup of tea is usually served at the end of the meal, as desserts are only reserved for special occasions.

Chopstick Hints

To truly experience a Chinese meal, you simply must use chopsticks! (You can purchase disposable chopsticks in the ethnic food section of your local grocery.) Hold the top stick with your thumb, middle, and forefinger (like you would hold a pencil) while balancing the bottom stick between your ring finger and the back of your thumb. Now grab the food between the sticks. This will definitely take some practice! In the meantime, follow these rules concerning chopstick etiquette:

1. Do not use the chopsticks as musical instruments on the dishes or the table.
2. Do not use the chopsticks to poke, prod, or stab your food.
3. Do not suck or chew on the chopsticks.
4. Never leave the chopsticks standing upright in a bowl of rice.
5. To eat rice, hold the bowl up with one hand and scoop the rice into your mouth with chopsticks.

Dan Hua Tang (Egg Drop Soup)

No need to use your chopsticks here! Spoons are acceptable when used with soup.

2 room temperature eggs, beaten
4 cups chicken stock
1 tsp salt
1 tsp sugar
2 tsp soy sauce
2 green onions, chopped (green parts only)

1. Bring chicken stock to a boil; reduce heat to low.
2. Slowly and carefully pour the eggs into the broth in a very thin stream. While pouring in the egg, hold a fork in your other hand and slowly stir the broth. Simmer for about 1 minute, and then remove from heat and cover for forty-five seconds.
3. Add salt, sugar, and soy sauce; stir. Serve topped with green onion.

Dan Juan (Egg Rolls)

2 T peanut oil
3 chicken breasts, chopped
3 garlic cloves, chopped
2 T soy sauce
1 cup bean sprouts
1 cup waterchestnuts, chopped
½ cup chives, chopped
1 small onion, chopped
¼ tsp ground ginger
½ lb egg roll skins, thawed if frozen
1 egg, beaten
peanut oil (for frying)

1. Heat the two tablespoons of peanut oil in the frying pan. Saute chicken, garlic, and soy sauce until chicken is browned. Add the bean sprouts, waterchestnuts, chives, onion, and ginger powder; stir fry for two minutes or until the bean sprouts are tender. Remove from heat; drain any excess liquid from pan.
2. Lay one egg roll skin on a flat surface. Place approximately ¾ cup of chicken mixture slightly below center of the egg roll. Fold up the bottom corner so it covers the mixture; fold the left and right corners toward the center so they overlap. Brush the top corner with egg, roll up the enclosed filling and seal. Repeat until you run out of filling.
3. Heat two inches of peanut oil to 250°F. Deep fry two egg rolls at a time until golden, about three minutes.

Lo Mein (Noodles)

Be sure to chop all of the ingredients into bite-size pieces. It is considered rude for a guest to ever have to cut anything at the table. You should be able to find oyster sauce in the Asian section at your grocery store. If not, substitute with soy sauce.

2 T soy sauce
1 garlic clove, minced
1 tsp cornstarch
1 T peanut oil
½ lb boneless chicken breasts, chopped
1 large carrot, sliced
3 sticks celery, chopped
4 oz mushrooms, sliced
8 oz thin egg noodles, cooked and drained
1 cup chicken broth
1 T oyster sauce
1 T cornstarch
1 T soy sauce

1. Mix soy sauce, garlic, and one teaspoon cornstarch in a small container. Add chicken and marinate in refrigerator for twenty minutes.
2. Heat the peanut oil in a wok or skillet on high heat. Stir fry the chicken and carrots for two minutes. Add the celery and mushrooms, and cook until the chicken is done. If you are cooking on high and everything is in small pieces, this should not take long at all, so be careful not to burn the food!
3. Whisk together the chicken broth, oyster sauce, corn starch, and soy sauce. Stir mixture into chicken; add noodles. Stir for two minutes, or until sauce is thickened. Serve.

- To announce the birth of a baby, the father sends boiled eggs that have been dyed red to family and friends. An even number means a boy, an odd number announces a girl.
- Fortune cookies originated in California, not China! Legend has it that a baker named David Jung created the cookie to hand out to homeless people and give them good fortunes.
- Chinese tradition forbids the use of forks or knives at the dinner table because these utensils resemble weapons.

Make More Than Dinner!

The British ruled over India, the world's second most populous nation, from the mid-1800s up until 1947. British soldiers and visitors to India returned home with a love for the spicy cuisine of the country. This love of Indian food has since spread all over the world.

Indian Eating Style

Indians believe that the best meals contain a combination of each of their six main flavor groups—sweet, sour, salty, spicy, bitter, and astringent. This helps each dining experience stay well-balanced. Food in India is often served at a low table, while everyone sits on low cushions or stools. Rather than serve the meal in courses, a host or hostess serves each dish at the same time. The meal is often served on a large platter, called a thali, with rice or bread in the middle, with the other dishes surrounding it. Indians generally eat with their hands—legend has it that the food tastes better that way.

Masala Chai (Spiced Tea)

Chai is the Indian word for tea. *Masala* means spice. Spiced tea is a common treat in India that is sold in roadside stalls all over the country. This version uses ingredients commonly available in the rest of the world.

2 cups water
1 cup milk
4 black tea bags
2 T sugar
1/4 tsp cardamom
1/4 tsp fennel
1/4 tsp ginger
1 tsp cinnamon
1/4 tsp cloves
1/2 tsp vanilla

1. Combine milk and water in a saucepan or tea kettle; bring to a boil. Remove from heat.

2. Add tea bags and remaining ingredients. Steep for five to six minutes. Remove tea bags; serve.

Naan

4 cups all-purpose flour
1 tsp baking powder
¼ tsp baking soda
1 tsp salt
1 egg, beaten
6 T plain yogurt
3 tablespoons butter, melted
1 cup milk
1 T poppy seeds

1. Stir together flour, baking powder, baking soda, and salt. Add the egg, yogurt, two tablespoons of the melted butter, and the milk. Knead well. Form into a ball; cover with a damp cloth and let rise in a warm place for two hours.
2. Preheat oven to 400°F. Divide dough into six balls. Roll out into ovals, about six inches long and one-fourth inch thick. Place on a greased cookie sheet. Brush with remaining butter and sprinkle with poppy seeds.
3. Bake for six to ten minutes or until golden brown.

Culture à la Carte

- The spiciness of Indian cuisine can be attributed to the ancient Indians. They believed that adding spices to your food was good for your digestive health.
- In some parts of the country, banana leaves are used as serving dishes!
- The main religion of India is Hinduism. Cows are holy in Hindu beliefs, so beef is generally not eaten in India.

Food Profile: Curry

India is the world's leading producer of spices. In India, each family would have their own blend of spices for cooking, even different blends for different dishes. Curry is the British word for these spice blends. (Over time, however, the term "curry" has come to mean nearly any Indian dish or item related to Indian cooking.) While you can buy premixed curry powder at any grocery store, a true Indian chef would never dream of doing this. They make their own curries from fresh, high-quality ingredients right before preparing the dish that requires it. You can make your own version of curry powder by grinding some of your favorite seasonings together and storing in an airtight container until ready to use. Keep experimenting until you find the perfect blend for your taste buds!

Murgh Kari (Chicken Curry)

Garam masala is a popular spice mixture used in Indian cooking. You can purchase it in the spice section at your local grocer, or you can make your own like they do in India by combining coriander, black pepper, cumin, cardamom, cinnamon, and cloves to taste.

2 lbs skinned chicken breasts
3 tsp salt, divided
½ cup vegetable oil
1 small onion, chopped
1 T minced garlic
1½ tsp ginger
1 tsp cumin
1 tsp turmeric
1 tsp coriander
1 tsp ground cayenne pepper
½ cup + 1 T water
1 (15 oz) can crushed tomatoes
2 T fresh cilantro, chopped
½ cup yogurt
1 tsp garam masala
1 T fresh lemon juice

1. Sprinkle chicken breasts with two teaspoons of the salt. In a large skillet, heat the oil over high heat. Brown chicken. Remove to plate and set aside.
2. Add the onions, garlic, and ginger to the remaining oil. Saute for eight minutes. Stir in the cumin, turmeric, coriander, cayenne, and one tablespoon of water. Add the tomatoes, one tablespoon of the cilantro, yogurt, and remaining teaspoon of salt.
3. Add the chicken and one-half cup water. Bring to a boil. Sprinkle with garam masala, lemon juice, and remaining cilantro. Cover skillet and simmer for twenty minutes.

Make More Than Dinner!

The small nation of Israel contains several different climates within its borders, allowing for a large variety of food cultivation. There is such an abundance of different foods that Israel is often referred to as "The Land Flowing with Milk and Honey." When Israel became a nation in 1948, an influx of Jewish immigrants returned to their homeland, bringing the cuisines of over eighty countries with them. Because of this, Israel's cuisine is a hodgepodge of recipes and flavors from all over the globe.

Tzimmes (Sweet Carrot Casserole)

2 large sweet potatoes, peeled and sliced
4 apples, peeled and chopped
5 carrots, peeled and sliced
½ cup small pitted prunes
juice and zest of 1 orange
honey
light brown sugar
cinnamon

1. Preheat oven to 350°F. Grease a large baking dish. Layer potatoes, carrots, apples, and prunes.
2. Add orange juice and zest. Drizzle with honey; sprinkle with cinnamon and brown sugar.
3. Cover with pierced foil. Bake for an hour and a half or until potatoes are tender.

Food Profile: Honey

Honey has been used as a sweetener for years. In fact, the first record of beekeeping activities can be traced back to the ancient Egyptians! Bees go through a lot of trouble to make the sweet stuff, pollinating plants along the way. They travel up to two miles from their hive to search for nectar at the speed of nearly fifteen miles per hour. It takes around two million trips to a flower just to make one pound of honey! One worker bee makes, on average, one twelfth of a teaspoon in its lifetime. Bees continue to return to the same type of flower to make their honey, hence the different kinds of honey — clover, orange blossom, etc. Each type of honey was made from the nectar of that type of flower.

Challah

Challah is a traditional Jewish braided bread. The word *challah* actually refers to a small portion of the dough which was taken from each batch of bread made by the Jews and given to the priests. All the small bits of dough were then combined to form a loaf for the priests, which ended up taking on the name of the small pieces, *challah.*

1 T sugar
1 package (1/4 oz) active dry yeast
1/2 cup warm water
3 T butter, melted
2 eggs
3 1/4 cups flour
olive oil
1 egg, beaten with 1 T water
poppy seeds

1. Combine sugar, yeast, and warm water. Let sit until foamy, about five minutes. Add flour, butter, and the two eggs. Stir until a dough forms. Turn out onto floured counter and knead until smooth, about five minutes. (To knead, fold the dough over, press it down with the heel of your hand, make a quarter turn, and repeat.)
2. Coat the inside of a large mixing bowl with olive oil. Add dough and turn to coat. Let rise for two and a half hours in a warm place. (The dough should double in size.)
3. Preheat oven to 375°F. Grease a cookie sheet. Punch down dough and divide into three equal portions. Form each portion into a rope just shorter than the cookie sheet. Lay the three ropes parallel on the cookie sheet. Braid the ropes together by crossing the first rope over the second, then the third rope over those, and repeat.
4. Brush with beaten egg and generously sprinkle with poppy seeds. Bake for thirty-five to forty-five minutes or until golden brown.

Kashruth are the Jewish dietary laws. These religious laws are adhered to in varying degrees among the people of Israel. Some, especially the religious leaders, follow the laws very strictly, while others disregard them completely. A dish or restaurant is considered kosher if it follows all of the rules exactly. Here are just a few:

- No pork or shellfish can be consumed.
- Meat and dairy products cannot be mixed. Strict adherents to this rule keep a separate set of dishes for meals containing meat and meals containing dairy products, such as milk or butter. They even have separate sinks to wash the dishes so that they never come in contact with the other.
- Only certain parts of the animal can be consumed, and no blood of the animal can be consumed. This complicates the butchering of an animal so much so that there are special kosher butchers trained to follow the laws correctly.

Cholent

Traditional Jewish laws prohibit doing any work, including cooking, on the Sabbath day. *Cholent* was originally created so that it could be prepared the day before Sabbath and cook all evening, thus being ready to eat the next morning. Those who strictly adhere to the Jewish religious laws would not even stir the dish once Sabbath day had began. You can customize this recipe by putting in any vegetables that may be left from another recipe, such as carrots, celery, turnips, parsnips, or leeks.

2 T vegetable oil
1 large onion, peeled and chopped
2 cloves garlic, minced
2 lbs beef brisket or chuck roast
1 T paprika
1 tsp salt
1 tsp pepper
2 cups dry mixed beans, soaked overnight and drained
1 cup barley
4 potatoes, peeled and diced
6 eggs

1. Preheat oven to 200°F. In a heavy pan, heat the oil to medium heat. Brown the meat with the onions, garlic, paprika, salt, and pepper. Transfer to a large baking dish. Cover with beans, barley, and potatoes. Gently add the eggs—yes, the whole egg, shell and all. Pour water over the dish until there is about one inch of water above the highest point.
2. Cover tightly with a lid or aluminum foil and bake for eighteen to twenty-four hours. (If you would like to cook this more quickly, cook it at 350°F for five or six hours.) Check the stew every few hours to make sure the water still covers the food.
3. Before serving, bring out the eggs and remove the shells. You can cut them in half and serve them as an appetizer or just put one on each plate. Slice the beef to serve.

Make More Than Dinner!

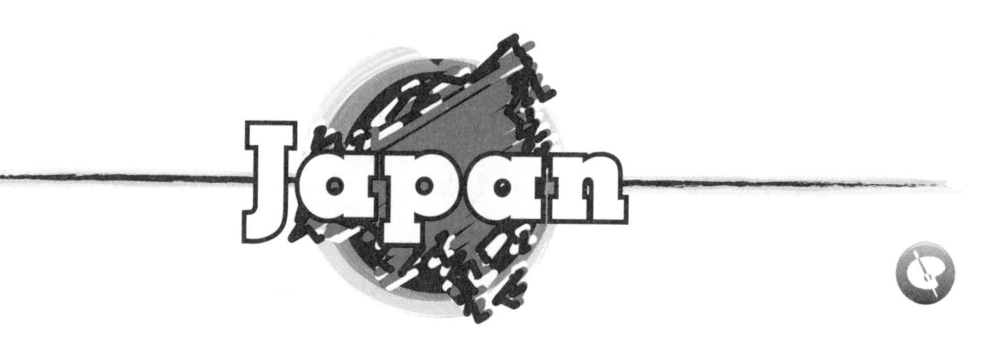

The islands of Japan remained somewhat isolated from most of the known world throughout the history of their civilization. This isolation left Japan with a cuisine mostly unaffected by other countries. Sushi, made with raw fish, is one example of a completely Japanese dish. The food of Japan contains a sparse amount of spice, instead focusing on the fresh, raw flavors of locally and seasonally available foods, such as seaweed, rice, and fish. Buddhism, the main religion of the Japanese, dictates that each meal contain as many of the following colors as possible: yellow, black, white, green, and red.

Dining In Japan

In Japan, all meals are served on a very low table, with everyone sitting on the floor. At the beginning of each meal, someone must say "Itadakimasu," which means "I shall receive." Japanese eat a little bit of each dish at a time. For example, you would not eat all of your rice, then all of your leeks. You would eat a portion of each dish and then start again eating a portion of each dish, always in equal proportions. White rice is served with every meal. Diners eat with chopsticks, following similar chopstick etiquette as the Chinese. At the end of each meal, someone must say, "Gochisosamedeshita," which roughly translates to "Thank you for this meal."

Yakinegi (Leeks)

4 leeks, trimmed of dark green parts and cut diagonally
1 tsp sesame oil
2 T soy sauce

1. Combine sesame oil and soy sauce in a skillet over medium heat.
2. Add leeks; saute until tender. Serve warm.

Sukiyaki

Sukiyaki is usually cooked right at the table, and everyone eats right out of the cooking dish. In Japan, you would dip each bite in raw, beaten eggs before eating! If you want to prepare this the Japanese way, cook everything in an electric skillet right on the kitchen table, but take extra care so that no one gets burned.

½ cup soy sauce
¼ cup sugar
½ cup beef broth
2 T vegetable oil
1 lb ribeye, sliced into thin strips
10 green onions, sliced
4 celery stalks, sliced
8 oz shiitake or button mushrooms, sliced
8 oz tofu, cubed
1 8 oz can bamboo shoots, drained

1. Mix soy sauce, sugar, and broth in a bowl and set aside. Heat vegetable over medium heat in a large skillet. Brown the meat, then add the remaining ingredients. Each ingredient is cooked in its own part of the skillet—it will be a tight squeeze! (You may have to divide it into two separate skillets.)

2. Add the broth mixture and cook for about seven minutes or until ingredients are tender. Serve straight from the skillet—no bowls or plates needed!

JAPANESE ETIQUETTE

- An empty plate signals that you want more food. If you are finished, always leave a little bit on your plate.
- It is never, ever polite to serve yourself food or drink. Someone must do this for you. You, in turn, always should make sure that those around you have full drinks and plates.
- Slurping of soup or noodles is acceptable, even expected!
- It is impolite to wear shoes at the dining table.

Daigakuimo (Candied Sweet Potato)

vegetable oil for frying
1 large sweet potato, thinly sliced
1/3 cup sugar
1 tsp soy sauce
2 T water
1 tsp sesame seeds

1. Coat the bottom of a skillet with a thin layer of vegetable oil. Heat to medium; add sweet potatoes. Stir frequently until sweet potatoes have browned. Remove to paper towels to drain.

2. Mix sugar, soy sauce, and water in a small saucepan. Stir over low heat until the mixture begins to thicken. Add sweet potatoes and stir briefly.

3. Sprinkle with sesame seeds. Serve warm.

- At a funeral, a bowl of rice is presented to the deceased person. The Japanese believe this gives the dead something to eat in the afterlife.
- "Gohan," the word for "rice," is also the word for "meal." This shows how important rice is to the Japanese!
- Squid is the most popular pizza topping in Japan!

Make More Than Dinner!

Food is very important to the people of Korea. In many cultures, people greet one another by saying, "How are you today?" In Korea, however, the common greeting is "Have you eaten?" In the past, a man's wealth was even based on how much rice he owned. South Korea is located between China and Japan, therefore sharing a very similar cuisine to both countries.

Hwa che

This deliciously different drink is popular in South Korea. You could easily adapt it to be made with any fruit and soda!

1 watermelon
Ginger ale
Sugar

1. Cut the watermelon into small chunks or make into balls with a melon baller. Divide into enough glasses for everyone you are serving. (There may be extra watermelon left for you to eat!)
2. Sprinkle sugar into each glass, then fill with ginger ale. Cover and chill until ready to serve.

Say What!

Shiksah: meal
Chonyok: dinner
Sohgohgi: beef
Pahp: rice
Bahng: bread
Mool: water
Sogoom: Salt
Hoo'choo: pepper
Subak: watermelon
Pa: green onions

Food Profile: Kimchi

The harsh winters of South Korea made creative ways of food preservation necessary in the past. One way that vegetables were preserved was by allowing them to ferment in special clay pots designed for the purpose. The result is kimchi, which is considered the national dish of Korea. Each kimchi mix is unique, but most contain some form of cabbage. Kimchi is usually served with every meal in Korea. You may be able to find kimchi in the Asian foods aisle of your local grocer.

Sanjuck

½ lb lean round steak, cubed
2 T sesame oil
1 T soy sauce
1 clove garlic, crushed
½ tsp sugar
¼ tsp chili powder
pepper
vegetable oil
8 oz button mushrooms, halved
12 green onions
2 eggs, beaten
flour

1. Combine sesame oil, soy sauce, garlic, sugar, and chili powder. Pepper to taste. Add beef and marinate in fridge for one hour.
2. Cover the bottom of a skillet with oil and heat. Trim onions to where the green leaves separate, then cut into half-inch sections. Thread onto skewers, alternating with beef and mushrooms.
3. Dip skewers in beaten egg, then in flour. Cook in heated oil until brown and crisp, about three minutes per side. Serve with rice.

- Koreans are often called "garlic eaters" by the Japanese. (Koreans love garlic, while most Japanese despise it.)
- In the past, Koreans dined using silver chopsticks because silver will change colors if the food is poisoned! In modern times, stainless steel chopsticks are used.
- Unlike the Chinese and Japanese, Koreans do not use chopsticks to eat their rice, but use spoons instead.

Ehoba Pak Jon

4 zucchini, sliced
1 tsp salt, divided
2 eggs, beaten
2 T flour
vegetable oil for frying

1. Put zucchini in a plastic container; sprinkle with salt. Let stand for ten minutes. Add flour, cover, and shake until zucchini is thoroughly coated.
2. Heat oil in a skillet to medium. Dip zucchini into egg and fry until golden brown, about one minute per side. Drain on paper towels. Serve warm with soy sauce for dipping.

Make More Than Dinner!

Europe

French cuisine is considered the most elegant of all international cuisines. It is the standard against which all others are measured. Many of the dishes require much time and energy in preparation. The dishes featured here are some of the simpler French fare.

Le Fromage (The Cheese)

The are nearly four hundred varieties of cheese in France—at least one for every day of the year! The French eat cheese with almost every meal. It is commonly served on a wooden board (much like a cutting board) with a small knife for cutting. It is usually accompanied by a loaf of French bread. You can serve one or a combination of the following French cheeses:

- *Camembert* is perhaps the most common cheese in France.
- *Brie* is widely available in the United States.
- *Chevre* is cheese made from goat's milk.
- *Roquefort* is a very popular blue cheese.

Soupe A L'Oignon (Onion Soup)

2 T butter
4 large onions, peeled and sliced
2 T flour
4 cups beef stock
salt
pepper
1 loaf French bread, sliced
1 cup shredded Swiss cheese

1. Preheat oven to 350°F. Melt butter in a large stock pot over medium heat. Add onions; cook until golden brown. Add flour and beef broth and bring to a boil. Reduce heat to low and simmer for twenty minutes.
2. Top French bread with cheese and bake until cheese is lightly browned. Ladle soup into bowls and top with French bread. Serve. Salt and pepper to taste.

Tomates (Tomatoes)

4 tomatoes, sliced in half
coarse salt
4 T fresh parsley, chopped
2 sprigs fresh thyme, chopped
2 garlic cloves, minced
olive oil
breadcrumbs

1. Preheat oven to 400°F. Remove and discard tomato cores. Place cut-side up in a large baking dish. Sprinkle with salt, parsley, thyme, and garlic. Drizzle with olive oil. Sprinkle with breadcrumbs.
2. Bake, uncovered, for thirty minutes. Serve warm.

- For luck, French brides break an egg on the doorstep of their new home before entering after the wedding.
- French fries did not originate in France, but in Belgium. The French, however, made them popular.
- Some French delicacies include snails, horse meat, lamb brains, and raw eel.

French Etiquette

- *It is always polite to bring a small gift for your hostess, but never carnations. (Carnations are usually reserved for funerals only.)*
- *Spoons and forks are placed face down. The blade of a knife should face the plate.*
- *The women are served first, from oldest to youngest. The men are served next in the same order.*
- *Everything at a French table is eaten with silverware — even fruit!*
- *Bread is not usually buttered in France. There is usually not a bread plate on the table because the bread is placed directly on the tablecloth.*
- *It is very impolite to season your food, especially if you do not even taste it first! It would be extremely rude to request a bottle of ketchup at a meal in France.*

Pain (Bread)

1½ cups warm water
1 (¼ oz) package active dry yeast
2 T sugar
2 T olive oil
1 tsp salt
4 cups bread flour

1. Combine water, yeast, and sugar in a mixing bowl. Let sit until foamy, about ten minutes. Stir in remaining ingredients. Continue stirring until a dough firms. Turn out onto a floured counter and knead until smooth, about ten minutes.
2. Place dough in a greased bowl and turn once to coat. Cover with a damp cloth and let rise until doubled, about one hour. Punch down dough. Divide into two equal portions and roll into long French loaves. Place on a greased baking sheet and cover with a damp cloth. Let rise until doubled again, about forty minutes.
3. Preheat oven to 400°F. Place loaves in oven and bake until golden brown, about eighteen to twenty minutes.

Food Profile: Tomatoes

The tomato is one of the world's most popular vegetables. (Well, it is technically a fruit, but most people eat it like a vegetable.) However, it was not always so popular. Tomatoes were originally cultivated by the Aztecs in Mexico. Europeans thought that they were poisonous because of their strong scent and similarities to other poisonous plants. Many people grew them for decorations. It was hundreds of years before the idea that tomatoes might be safe to eat started to take hold. Now tomatoes are popular everywhere, with nearly half of the tomatoes grown used to make ketchup and tomato sauce.

Make More Than Dinner!

For many years, especially during Nazi rule, German families struggled to put food onto the table. Because of this, much of German cuisine is simply prepared and made with affordable ingredients. Their food is similar to that of other Eastern European nations.

Bretzels (Soft Pretzels)

Legend has it that *bretzels* were first given to German children as rewards for learning their prayers—hence the shape of praying hands.

1 tsp salt
1 T sugar
1 package (¼ oz) active dry yeast
1½ cups warm water
3½ cups flour
vegetable oil
1 egg, beaten with 1 T water
coarse salt

1. Stir together salt, sugar, yeast, and warm water. Let sit until foamy, about five minutes. Stir in flour until it forms into a dough. Turn out onto a floured counter and knead for seven to eight minutes. (To knead, fold the dough over, press it down with the heel of your hand, make a quarter turn, and repeat.)
2. Coat the inside of a large bowl with vegetable oil. Add the dough, turning to coat with oil. Cover with plastic wrap and let rise for one to two hours in a warm place. (The dough should double in size.)
3. Cover two cookies sheets with parchment paper. Punch down dough and divide into twelve pieces. Form each section of dough into a rope about twelve inches long. Twist each rope into a pretzel shape. (Cross the ends to form a loop; twist the crossed ends and fold down to the loop.) Cover loosely with plastic wrap and let rise for another hour.
4. Preheat oven to 425°F. Brush pretzels with beaten egg and sprinkle with coarse salt. Bake the pretzels for twelve to fifteen minutes or until lightly browned. Serve with mustard.

Bratwurst and Sauerkraut

2 T butter
1 small onion, chopped
1 clove garlic, minced
4 cups sauerkraut, drained
3 potatoes, peeled and sliced
1½ cups water
½ cup apple juice
1 T brown sugar
1 tsp chicken bouillon
1 large apple, peeled and sliced
1 lb. bratwurst, pierced

1. In a large skillet, saute onion and garlic in butter until onion is translucent. Add sauerkraut, potatoes, water, apple juice, brown sugar, and chicken bouillon. Bring to a boil.
2. Add bratwurst to sauerkraut. Reduce heat; simmer until potatoes begin to soften, about twenty minutes.
3. Add the apple, cover and cook for ten minutes until apples are tender. Serve.

- Germans often eat their French fries with mayonnaise.
- The Easter tradition of decorating eggs first began in Germany.
- German couples in the Middle Ages filled their pockets with the spice cumin for their wedding ceremony because it was believed to bring good luck and years of being faithful to each other.

Food Profile: Sauerkraut

Sauerkraut means "sour cabbage" in German. It is made by combining shredded cabbage and salt and allowing it to ferment for several days. This method of preserving cabbage was used to provide food through the long German winters. Sauerkraut is very high in vitamin C and was often taken on sea voyages as a treatment for scurvy.

Apfelstrudel (Apple Strudel)

6 sheets phyllo dough (from an 8 oz package)
½ cup melted butter
¼ cup breadcrumbs
2 apples, cored and sliced
½ cup raisins
¼ cup slivered almonds
¼ cup sugar
½ tsp cinnamon
¼ tsp nutmeg
⅛ tsp ginger
1 egg + 1 tsp water, beaten
Powdered sugar

1. Preheat oven to 400°F. Place a damp kitchen towel on counter. Cover with one sheet of phyllo dough. (If using frozen dough, be sure that it is thawed.) Brush with melted butter and sprinkle with breadcrumbs. Top with another layer of dough. Brush with butter and sprinkle with breadcrumbs; add another layer of dough.
2. Leaving a half-inch margin around the edges of the dough, cover with half the apples, raisins, and almonds. Mix sugar with cinnamon, nutmeg, and ginger. Generously sprinkle over dough. Sprinkle with breadcrumbs. Very gently roll up strudel like a jelly roll, and seal ends shut. Brush with melted butter and beaten egg. Sprinkle with breadcrumbs. Transfer to a greased baking sheet, using the towel to aid you if necessary.
3. Repeat steps one and two to create a second strudel. Once both strudels are on the baking sheet, transfer to the oven. Bake for twenty to twenty five minutes—the strudel will be dark brown. To serve, sprinkle with powdered sugar.

Say What!
Vorspeise: appetizer
Suppe: soupe
Hauptspeise: main course
Beilagen: side dish
Abendessen: dinner
Brot: bread
Kartofel: Potato
Lotfel: spoon

Make More Than Dinner!

The island of Great Britain is made up of England, Scotland, and Wales. Because the British once ruled most of the known world, their cuisine has tastes from all over, from Chinese tea to Indian curry.

Have A Spot O'Tea

There are many things that one might associate with Britain, but perhaps the most famous is the ritual of serving tea in the afternoon. This Tea, traditionally served around four o'clock in the afternoon, began with the seventh Duchess of Bedford, England, who thought it would be a good way to bridge the long span between breakfast and dinner. (Lunch was not commonly served.) The tea includes light refreshments served in three courses: savory sandwiches, scones, and dessert. Serve this meal with different English teas, such as Earl Grey. You may wish to serve some fresh fruit as well. For dessert, try serving cookies or cake.

Cucumber Sandwiches

If you are serving lots of people, serve different types of sandwiches in addition to this one. Other sandwiches that might commonly be served at Tea in Britain would be made with tuna, ham, turkey, or chicken salad. Just be sure to trim off the crusts and cut into small triangles.

1 cucumber, peeled and thinly sliced
8 slices white bread
Salted butter, softened

1. Spread butter on one side of each bread slice. Place cucumber slices on half of the bread slices in a single layer.
2. Top with another slice of bread, butter facing the cucumbers.
3. Trim and discard bread crusts; cut each sandwich into four small triangles. Serve.

Mushroom Turnovers

8 oz button mushrooms, chopped
2 T fresh parsley, minced
2 T onion, chopped
3 T butter, divided
1 8 oz can refrigerated crescent roll dough
fresh grated parmesan cheese
sesame seeds

1. Preheat oven to 375°F. In a skillet, saute the mushrooms, parsley, and onion in 2 tablespoons of the butter over medium heat until onions are translucent.
2. Cut the dough into twelve squares or triangles. Place a small spoonful of mushroom mixture on one side of each square. Top mixture with a sprinkle of parmesan cheese. Fold over and seal using the tines of a fork.
3. Melt the remaining butter and brush onto turnovers. Sprinkle with sesame seeds.
4. Bake for ten to fifteen minutes or until golden brown. Serve warm.

TEA TIME ETIQUETTE

- *Pick up the cup and saucer together, holding one with the left hand and the other with the right.*
- *Milk is poured in the teacup after the tea.*
- *Never hit the side of the cup while stirring.*
- *Never leave your spoon in the cup.*
- *Never wave your cup around in the air.*
- *To properly eat a scone, it should be cut in half. Cover one half with your toppings of choice, then eat and repeat with the other half.*

Scones

This is a basic scone recipe. You can customize by adding berries, dried fruits, or even chocolate chips! Serve scones with an assortment of jams, preserves, and marmalades.

2 cups all-purpose flour
⅓ cup sugar
2 tsp baking powder
⅛ tsp salt
⅓ cup unsalted butter
1 egg, beaten
1 tsp vanilla
½ cup heavy whipping cream
Topping: 1 egg, beaten + 1 T heavy whipping cream

1. Preheat oven to 375°F. In a large bowl, stir together flour, sugar, baking powder, and salt. Cut in the butter and blend until the mixture resembles course crumbs. If you are adding any extras, such as chocolate chips or berries, add ⅓ cup now.
2. In a small bowl, combine the cream, beaten egg, and vanilla, then add to flour mixture. Stir gently then knead dough on a lightly floured surface. Roll the dough into a circle about 1½ inch thick. Cut into eight triangles.
3. Brush scones with topping; bake for fifteen minutes or until lightly browned.

- At one time, plum pudding was outlawed in Britain because it was so richly delicious, it was believed to be a sin to eat it.
- The fourth Earl of Sandwich, England, John Montague, is credited with inventing the sandwich. He was an avid gambler who would eat his meat between two slices of bread rather than have to take a break from gambling to eat!
- Sausages in Britain are called "bangers." This name originates in World War II, where the high water content of sausage (made so to stretch the supply) often caused the sausages to explode while cooking.

Make More Than Dinner!

Ireland is often called "The Emerald Isle" because of its lush, green pastures which are visible all along the country's coastline. The food of Ireland is hearty and practical, made with whatever is readily available.

Celebrate St. Patrick's Day

You may choose to eat your Irish meal on St. Patrick's Day, March 17. St. Patrick is known for converting the Celtic people of Ireland to Christianity. He is honored on this day by the Irish and the rest of the world through all kinds of festivities and parades. In recent times, St. Patrick's Day has developed into a celebration of Irish culture, not just St. Patrick. Green is the color typically associated with St. Patrick's day (because of the greenness of Ireland), so be sure to decorate your table with all things green!

Stew

2 lb. lamb stewing meat, cubed
4 cups water
3 potatoes, peeled and diced
3 carrots, sliced
1 turnip, chopped
1 onion, chopped
3 T fresh parsley, chopped
2 tsp salt
½ tsp pepper
1 bay leaf
¼ cup cold water
2 T flour

1. Combine lamb and water in a large soup pot. Bring to a boil. Reduce heat to low. Cover and simmer until lamb is tender, between one and two hours.
2. Add potatoes, carrots, turnip, onion, parsley, salt, pepper, and bay leaf. Continue simmering until vegetables are tender, about thirty minutes.
3. In a small bowl, stir together water and flour until smooth. Add to stew. Bring to a boil. Simmer for ten minutes, stirring frequently, until stew is thickened. Serve hot.

Champ

"Champ" is the name for this Irish version of mashed potatoes, although in some parts of the country, it is called "Poundies."

4 large potatoes, peeled
water
4 green onions, chopped
1 cup milk
½ cup butter

1. Place potatoes in a pot and cover with water. Bring to a boil. Boil until potatoes are tender, about twenty minutes. Drain.
2. In a separate saucepan, combine milk, green onions, and ¼ cup of the butter. Heat over low heat until onions are soft.
3. Combine potatoes and green onion mix in a medium mixing bowl. Mash. To serve, divide into four bowls. Make a well on top of each mound of potatoes and top with a tablespoon of butter. Serve hot.

Culture à la Carte

- The Irish eat on average 300 pounds of potatoes per person every year – more than any other country in Europe.
- An average potato is 80% water.
- The tradition of carving pumpkins for Halloween began in Ireland.

Food Profile: Potatoes

The potato is a staple in Irish cooking. It first arrived in Ireland in the sixteenth century, from Sir Walter Raleigh in Virginia. The Irish quickly developed a dependence on the potato, resulting in the Potato Famine, which occurred in the 1840s. Nearly one-fifth of the country's population died from starvation when the potato crop was destroyed by disease. Over two million Irish left the country in search of food. Because of this great outpouring of immigrants from the Emerald Isle, many families all over the world can trace their heritage back to Ireland.

Soda Bread

This bread is called "Soda Bread" because it uses baking soda rather than yeast to help to rise.

3 cups flour
⅓ cup sugar
1 T baking powder
1 tsp salt
1 tsp baking soda
2 cups buttermilk
¼ cup butter, melted
1 egg, beaten

1. Preheat oven to 325°F. Stir together dry ingredients. Add buttermilk, butter, and egg. Stir well.
2. Place dough in a greased bread pan. Bake until a toothpick inserted in the middle comes out clean, about one hour.

Make More Than Dinner!

Italian cuisine is world-famous for its tasty and filling meals. Some Italian dishes have become more popular abroad than in their home country of Italy. For example, Americans consume more pizza per year than Italians! Italian meals are served in small portions, one dish at a time. This helps lengthen meals from a hurried dinner with little conversation into a family event filled with lots of chatter!

Pizza Margherita

Pizza is one of Italy's most famous dishes. This simple pizza is a classic recipe. It is named for Italy's Queen Margherita, who visited the city of Naples in 1889. The pizza maker there created a special pizza just for her with the colors of the Italian flag—red tomatoes, white mozzarella, and green basil.

1 package 10 oz refrigerated pizza dough
1/3 cup tomato sauce
3 tomatoes, sliced
1 cup fresh mozzarella, sliced
1/4 cup fresh basil leaves, torn

1. Preheat oven to 400°F. Roll pizza dough out thinly and divide into four equal sections. (Pizzas in Italy are normally served in individual sizes.)
2. Spoon tomato sauce over each pizza. Top with sliced tomato, basil leaves, and mozzarella. Bake for eight to eleven minutes or until cheese begins to brown.

ITALIAN COURSES

- *Antipasto: the appetizers*
- *Primo: the first course, usually a soup*
- *Secondo: the second course, usually a small serving of meat, served with contorno, a side dish*
- *Dulce: dessert, often just pieces of fruit*
- *Caffe: coffee, served after every meal*

Minestrone

There is no exact recipe for minestrone, a classic Italian soup. Each region of Italy varies in their interpretation of the dish, and the exact measurements and ingredients may vary drastically from family to family. Using this recipe as a basic guide, add ingredients your family will like and leave out those that they wouldn't. Remember to discard the dark green part of the leeks.

¼ cup extra-virgin olive oil
2 medium leeks, trimmed and sliced
2 medium carrots, peeled and chopped
1 medium onion, peeled and chopped
1 clove garlic, minced
1 celery stalk, chopped
6 cups beef stock
1 medium potato, peeled and diced
1 medium zucchini, diced
3 cups tightly packed spinach leaves, chopped
1 28 oz can whole tomatoes, drained and chopped
½ cup rotini pasta
salt
fresh parmesan cheese

1. Heat the olive oil in a large stock pot. Add the leeks, carrots, onion, garlic, and celery; sauté over medium heat until vegetables are tender, around ten minutes.
2. Add the beef stock, potato, zucchini, spinach, and tomatoes. Bring to a boil; reduce the heat and simmer for one hour.
3. Stir in the pasta and salt to taste. Continue cooking until pasta is tender, around fifteen minutes. Serve with freshly grated parmesan cheese.

ITALIAN ETIQUETTE

- *Never place your hands on your lap; they should remain visible at all times.*
- *Dine with your fork in your left hand and your knife in your right. (Do the opposite if you are left-handed.)*
- *The female guest of honor is served first, followed by the male guest of honor. The host and hostess are always served last.*
- *When asked to pass the salt, set it beside the person asking for it. Never place it directly in their hand.*

Panna Cotta (Cooked Cream)

Panna Cotta can be eaten plain or topped with fresh fruit—strawberries, raspberries, peaches, cherries, or pears. For even more flavor, top the fruit with hot fudge sauce.

1/3 cup milk
1 envelope (.25 oz) unflavored gelatin
2 1/2 cups heavy cream
1/2 cup white sugar
1 1/2 tsp vanilla extract

1. Stir together milk and gelatin in a small bowl; set aside.
2. In a medium pan, combine cream and sugar over medium heat. Bring to a boil, then add gelatin mixture. Cook, stirring constantly, for two minutes. Remove from heat; add vanilla.
3. Pour into four bowls and allow to cool, uncovered. After cooling is completed, cover and refrigerate for four hours or overnight.

- Pizza is served all over the world, with different regions having their own unique toppings: ginger and tofu in India, coconut in Costa Rice, peas in Brazil, and mockba (a seafood medley made with tuna, sardines, salmon, and anchovies) in Russia.
- The average Italian consumes fifty-five pounds of pasta a year!
- Minestra, from which Minestrone gets its name, means "minister" in Italian. Priests would minestra to the poor by providing bowls of soup just like Minestrone.

Make More Than Dinner!

Holland's staple food is the potato. It is served with nearly every meal. Holland is also famous for their cheeses, such as Gouda and Edam. A perfect centerpiece for your meal would be a bouquet of tulips, the most famous Dutch flower.

Acar Bening (Cucumber Salad)

1 large cucumber, peeled and thinly sliced
1 tsp salt
1 T vinegar
½ tsp sugar
1 green onion, sliced
nutmeg

1. Sprinkle cucumber slices with salt. Let sit for two hours. Rinse off salt.
2. Combine cucumber, vinegar, sugar, and green onion in a bowl. Sprinkle with nutmeg. Chill until ready to serve.

Say What!

Aardappel: potato
Peen: carrot
Erwten: peas
Uien: onion
Prei: leek
Komkomer: cucumber
Zout: salt
Peper: pepper

Olliebollen

These are a type of doughnut traditionally served on New Year's Eve.

1/4 cup warm water
1 pkg active dry yeast
1/3 cup sugar
1/2 cup warm milk
1/2 tsp salt
3 eggs
3 1/3 cups flour
1 T cinnamon
1 large apple, peeled and chopped
1/2 cup raisins
vegetable oil for frying
powdered sugar

1. Stir together water, yeast, and 1/3 cup sugar. Let sit until foamy, about five minutes.
2. Add milk, salt, eggs, flour, cinnamon, apple, and raisins. Knead well. Place in a greased bowl, cover with a cloth, and let rise for two hours in a warm place. (The dough should double in size.)
3. Preheat a deep fryer to 350°F. (If you don't have a deep fryer, heat two inches of vegetable oil on the stove in a deep pan.) Punch down dough and divide into twelve balls. Fry in batches until golden brown. To serve, sprinkle with powdered sugar.

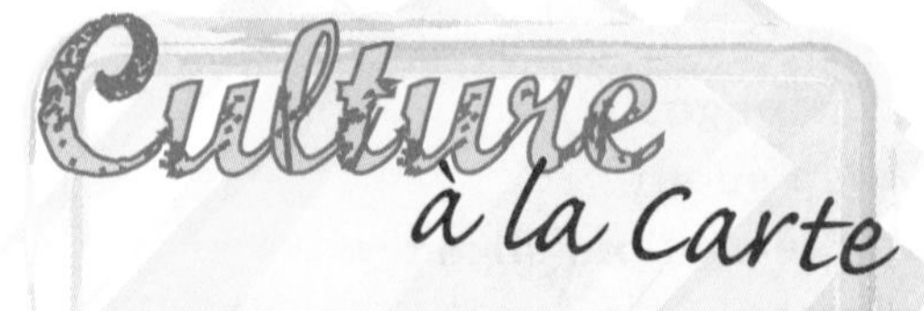

- Kids in Holland often eat chocolate sprinkles on their breakfast toast!
- A popular Dutch fast food is raw herring.
- Carrots naturally grow in nearly every color of the rainbow. Orange carrots first became popular in sixteenth century Holland, where farmers grew them in honor of the ruling family, the House of Orange.

Erwtensoep (Pea Soup)

2 cups dried split green peas
4 slices thick sliced bacon, cut into squares
1 tsp salt
water
2 potatoes, peeled and chopped
2 celery stalks, sliced
3 leeks, sliced (white parts only)
2 tsp thyme
¼ tsp pepper
1 lb. skinless kielbasa sausage, sliced

1. Combine peas, bacon, and salt in a large stock pot. Add enough water to cover ingredients and bring to a boil. Reduce heat, place lid on pot, and simmer for fifteen minutes.
2. Add potatoes, celery, leeks, thyme, and pepper. Continue to simmer for twenty more minutes.
3. Add sausage and cook for fifteen more minutes. If the soup is thin, continue to simmer until it thickens up. Serve hot.

Make More Than Dinner!

Russia

During the 18th century, it became popular for Russian nobility to import French chefs to cook in their kitchens. Thus, much of Russian cooking has ties to French cuisine. Russians have also learned to adapt to their extended winter season with hearty food made from ingredients that store well, especially root vegetables like beets, carrots, and potatoes.

Borscht (Beet Soup)

To turn this soup into a one pot meal, add a pound of cubed beef stew meat in step one.

2 T butter
1 cup diced tomatoes
1 beet, peeled and grated
1 small onion, chopped
1 green pepper, seeded and chopped
2 cloves garlic, minced
4 cups beef broth
3 potatoes, peeled and chopped
2 cups shredded cabbage
3 carrots, peeled and sliced
1 parsnip, peeled and sliced
½ T sugar
½ tsp black pepper

1. Melt butter over medium heat in a large stock pot. Add tomatoes, beet, onion, green pepper, and garlic. Cook until onions are soft.
2. Add beef broth, potatoes, cabbage, carrots, parsnip, sugar, and black pepper. Bring to a boil. Reduce heat and simmer until vegetables are tender, about twenty minutes. If desired, serve with a spoonful of sour cream and sprinkle with minced dill.

Say What!
Duhovka: oven
Goroh: peas
Grib: mushroom
Ponchik: doughnut
Vilka: fork
Vishnya: cherry
Savtrak: breakfast

Medianyky (Honey Cookies)

These honey cookies are served around Christmas time.

2 cups flour
½ tsp cinnamon
¼ tsp cloves
¼ tsp ginger
¼ tsp nutmeg
½ cup powdered sugar
1 tsp baking powder
1 egg
½ cup honey
1 egg + 1 T water, beaten
¼ cup slivered almonds

1. Preheat oven to 350°F. Stir together, flour, spices, sugar, and baking powder. Add egg and honey until a stiff dough forms.
2. Roll out dough to about one-half inch thick. Cut into desired shapes with cookies cutters. Top with almonds and brush with beaten egg.
3. Place on greased baking sheet. Bake for thirteen to fifteen minutes; let cool.

Food Profile: Beets

Beets, featured in the recipe for Borscht, are a popular item on menus all over Russia. Beets are high in vitamin C, and have been used throughout the centuries to treat a variety of illnesses — from fevers to poor digestion. The root of the beet is what usually comes to mind when we hear "beet," but actually the green leafy tops are also edible. They can be used in recipes as a replacement to any green, whether it be kale, collard, or even cabbage.

The smaller the beet, the more tender it will be. Extremely large beets may be too tough too eat. They should keep for two to four weeks in the refrigerator. (The green tops will not keep longer than a week.) To remove beet stains from your hands, rub with lemon juice, then rinse thoroughly.

Beef Stroganoff

Beef Stroganoff was originally served with fried potatoes, but in modern times it is usually served with egg noodles. Pick one to serve with, or try a little of both.

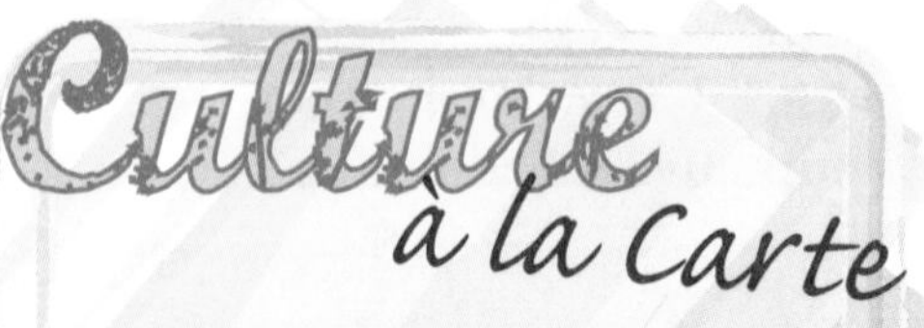

- In the United States, beet juice is often used to give pink lemonade its color.
- Beef stroganoff was named for a famous Russian, Count Pavel Stroganov, even though he did not invent the dish. He simply popularized it by frequently serving it at his elaborate dinner parties.
- A popular Russian saying is, "No dinner without bread." The Russians love their bread, especially dark varieties such as rye.

2 T butter
1 large onion, peeled and chopped
8 oz mushrooms, chopped
1 lb. ribeye, sliced into thin strips
2 cups sour cream
salt
pepper
fresh dill, chopped

1. Heat butter over medium heat. Saute onions and mushrooms until onions begin to soften.
2. Add beef and saute until meat is browned on all sides. Add sour cream, and salt and pepper to taste. Simmer six or seven minutes or until cream has thickened. To serve, sprinkle with dill.

Make More Than Dinner!

The Spanish have a very different eating schedule from most of the world. A typical day is made up of several snacks and smaller meals. A standard schedule would be: breakfast at 8 a.m., brunch at 11 a.m., snack at 1 p.m., lunch at 3 p.m., a snack at 5 p.m., snacks again at 8 p.m., and dinner at 10 p.m. Eat Spanish-style for a day and see how you like it!

A Taste Of "Tapas"

"Tapas" are small little Spanish appetizers. Served in both homes and restaurants, they are popular all over Spain and are slowly gaining popularity around the rest of the world. Perhaps the popularity of tapas is why the Spanish do so much snacking throughout the day! You can serve your own with a meal or, with enough variety, in place of a meal. Some ideas include raw vegetables, olives, cheese, small sandwiches, or meatballs. Anything bite-sized and delicious will make a great tapa!

Gazpacho

6 large tomatoes, chopped
1 green pepper, seeded and chopped
1 onion, peeled and chopped
1 large cucumber, peeled and chopped
2 garlic cloves, peeled and minced
4 T red wine vinegar
1 tsp sugar
¼ tsp tarragon
½ cup cold water

1. Combine all ingredients in a blender, and blend until smooth.
2. Cover and chill for two hours or overnight.
3. Serve cold. If desired, garnish with croutons and diced cucumbers.

Torrijes (Bread Pudding)

4 slices white bread, cut into strips
½ cup milk
1 egg, beaten
2 T butter
¼ cup honey

1. Preheat the oven to 325°F. Soak the bread in milk for five minutes. While the bread is soaking, heat the butter in a skillet.
2. Dip bread pieces in egg and then fry in butter until golden brown on both sides.
3. Place in a greased casserole dish, top with honey, and bake for twenty minutes. Serve warm or cold. Sprinkle with cinnamon sugar if desired.

- It is a Spanish tradition to eat a grape each time the clock chimes midnight on New Year's Eve – that's a dozen grapes to ring in the New Year!
- The average life span of an olive tree is five hundred years, although some trees are nearly two thousand years old.
- It takes nearly two thousand pounds of olives to make just fifty gallons of olive oil.

Food Profile: The Olive

Olives are the oldest tree grown by man on record. There are numerous references to this important evergreen all through history — from the Bible to Homer's Odyssey to the walls of ancient Egyptian tombs. The olive branch symbolizes peace, which is why it was used in the first Olympic games — the branch as a burning torch and the leaves as a crown for the winners.

Spain is the world's leading producers of olives, most of which is used in the production of olive oil. Olives straight from the tree are inedible; they must first be treated to remove the bitterness. Green olives have yet to ripen to their full black color. However, just because an olive is black does not mean it is ripe — many commercially available olives have been chemically blackened because allowing the olive to ripen on the tree is a long process.

Paella

1 lb chicken, diced
5 T olive oil
8 cups water
1 onion, peeled and chopped
1 red pepper, seeded and chopped
1 garlic clove, minced
2 tomatoes, chopped
1 cup long grain rice
1 cup canned peas
½ lemon, juiced
1 sprig thyme, chopped
1 sprig rosemary, chopped
1 T chopped parsley
¼ tsp turmeric
salt
pepper

1. Brown chicken in three tablespoons of olive oil over medium heat. Add water, bring to a boil. Reduce heat; simmer for thirty minutes.
2. In a separate skillet, heat remaining olive oil. Saute onion, red pepper, and garlic until onion begins to soften. Add tomatoes, saute for three more minutes.
3. Add onion mix to chicken. Also add rice, peas, lemon juice, herbs, and turmeric. Salt and pepper to taste. Bring mixture to a boil. Continue boiling for ten minutes. Reduce heat to low; simmer until all the liquid has evaporated. Serve warm.

Make More Than Dinner!

North America

Canada is second only to Russia in land mass. This large area is home to a varied climate. The culture of Canada is a mixture of the British and French people who settled the land. The influences of these cultures are evident in the hearty fare of these cultures.

Wild Rice

Wild rice is a native Canadian crop, growing along the shores of streams and ponds. If unable to purchase plain wild rice, try buying it mixed with long grain rice for this recipe.

1 cup wild rice
2 T butter
½ cup mushrooms, sliced
1 small onion, diced
1 celery stick, chopped
1 T fresh thyme, chopped
1 garlic clove, crushed
2 T fresh parsley, chopped
salt
pepper

1. Prepare rice according to package directions. Set aside.
2. Heat the butter in a skillet over medium heat. Add onion, celery, mushrooms, garlic, and thyme; saute until soft. Add the parsley. Stir ingredients into rice. Add salt and pepper to taste. Serve warm.

Maple Chicken

4 boneless, skinless chicken breasts
½ cup pure maple syrup
1 T fresh parlsey, chopped
1 T fresh thyme, chopped
1 T fresh sage, chopped
1 onion, chopped
1 cup chicken stock

1. Preheat oven to 350°F. Place chicken in an oven safe baking dish. Drizzle with maple syrup.
2. Stir together remaining ingredients. Pour over chicken. Bake for forty-five minutes. Serve warm.

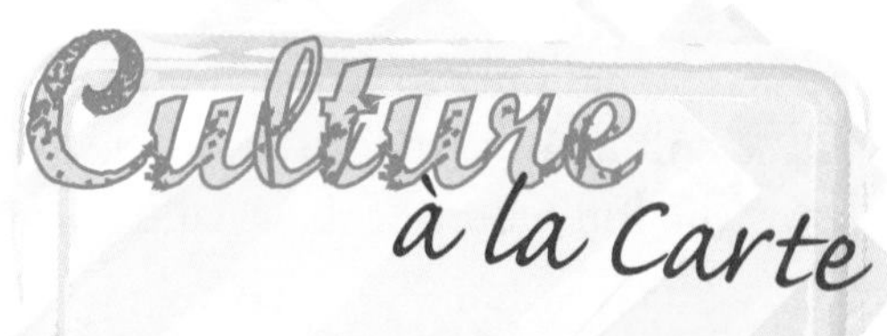

- Native Canadian recipes included ingredients like reindeer, skunk, polar bear, and porcupine.
- Fiddleheads are the first tender shoots of ferns. They are a Canadian delicacy!
- Canada produces nearly eighty percent of the world's maple syrup.

Food Profile: Maple Syrup

Maple syrup is produced from the sap of maple trees. It is harvested by drilling a hole in the tree and allowing the sap to drain out. The sap is then boiled until the extra liquid has evaporated, forming a syrup. It takes anywhere from forty to fifty gallons of sap to make one gallon of syrup. Maple syrup naturally comes in different shades. The first sap that drains from the tree is the lightest; it becomes darker the longer that it drains. Maple syrup will last the longest if stored in the refrigerator.

Blueberry Crisp

4 cups fresh or frozen blueberries
1/3 cup sugar
2 tsp lemon juice
4 T butter, softened
1/3 cup brown sugar
1/3 cup flour
3/4 cups quick-cooking oats

1. Preheat oven to 375°F. Place blueberries on the bottom of a baking dish. Sprinkle with sugar and lemon juice.
2. In a separate bowl, combine butter, brown sugar, flour, and oats. Spread over blueberries.
3. Bake for thirty to thirty-five minutes, or until top is golden. Serve with vanilla ice cream or whipped cream.

Make More Than Dinner!

Guatemala is the most populated country in Central America. Over fifty percent of Guatemalans are native to the country, descendants of the Mayan Indians. The food in Guatemala is a tasty blend of the native cuisine and that of Spanish and other European explorers. Dig in!

Grow a Pineapple!

You can grow your own pineapple at home! Follow these steps, keeping in mind that it might take more than one try to get a plant to take root. To bear a fruit the size that you see in the grocery store, the plant will have to be around six feet high. However, your house plant may bear a smaller fruit in around two years.

1. Grab a pineapple's leafy top with a firm grip. Twist. The leaves should come loose with a bit of the stalk. Remove the two bottom layer of leaves. Place in a cool, dark place to dry for three days.

2. Fill a glass with water and insert the pineapple stalk. Wait a few weeks until you see roots begin to grow, adding more water as needed.

3. Plant the stalk in a medium pot with potting soil. Water and place in a sunny window. (If you live in a very warm climate, you can grow your pineapple outdoors.)

4. Water once a week. Transplant to a bigger pot if it outgrows the one that it is in. Watch your pineapple grow!

Pollo y Piña (Chicken and Pineapple)

2 lb boneless chicken thighs
1 (16 oz) can unsweetened sliced pineapple OR
1 fresh pineapple, peeled, cored, and sliced
2 cups chicken broth
2 onions, chopped
2 garlic cloves, chopped
¼ tsp cloves
¼ tsp cinnamon
2 bay leaves
2 T white vinegar
1 tsp salt
1 tsp pepper
2 tomatoes, chopped

1. Preheat oven to 350°F. Combine all ingredients except tomatoes in a large baking dish.
2. Bake for thirty minutes, uncovered. Add tomatoes and continue baking for another thirty minutes. Serve.

Plåtanos de Bakeed (Baked Bananas)

4 bananas, peeled and sliced
2 T butter
3 T honey
2 T lemon juice

1. Preheat oven to 350°F. Place bananas in a greased baking dish. Add butter, honey, and lemon juice.
2. Bake for fifteen minutes, stirring halfway through. Serve plain or with nuts as an accompaniment to ice cream or yogurt.

Food Profile: Pineapple

The pineapple is the international symbol of hospitality. It is native to Central America, and was brought back to Europe by Christopher Columbus in 1493. Since then, it has become popular all over the world. A pineapple plant takes two years to bear fruit, and most plants produce only two fruits in their lifetime.

To select the perfect pineapple, choose one that is heavy for its size with no bruising or brown spots on the skin. The leaves should be bright green with no signs of wilting. If the pineapple is ripe, the bottom leaves should come out easily when gently pulled. If you have trouble peeling the pineapple, try slicing it into rings first. Then simply cut away the peel and core from the rings.

Sopa Del Pepino (Cucumber Soup)

1 T vegetable oil
4 cucumbers, peeled and chopped
1 onion, chopped
1 red bell pepper, seeded and diced
2 cups chicken broth
¼ cup plain yogurt
1 bunch fresh parsley, chopped

1. Saute cucumbers, onion, and pepper in vegetable oil until tender. Add chicken broth; bring to a boil.
2. Simmer for ten minutes. Puree soup in batches in a blender or food processor.
3. Serve warm with a tablespoon of yogurt in each bowl. Garnish with chopped parsley.

- The fibers in pineapple leaves are sometimes used by the people of Guatemala to make rope and fabric.
- The pineapple got its named from European explorers who thought that it resembled a pinecone.
- The ancient Mayans believed that chocolate was the food of the gods.

Make More Than Dinner!

Jamaica is the third largest island in the Caribbean. While you may not have tasted Jamaican food, you have probably heard Jamaican music. Reggae, a form of music, was developed on this island in the 1960's and has since become popular all over the world. Be sure to track down some reggae for your Jamaican dinner!

Ting

Ting is a popular Jamaican soda. This recipe tastes similar to the refreshing soft drink. If it is too tangy for your tastes, you can always tame it down with a few spoonfuls of sugar.

2 cups lemon-lime soda (such as 7-Up® or Sprite®)
2 cups grapefruit juice

1. Combine ingredients. Chill.
2. Serve with crushed ice.

Jerk Seasoning

You can buy Jamaican jerk seasoning in the spice aisle at your local grocery, or you can make your own following this recipe. All spices should be dried and ground.

1 T allspice
1 T sugar
1 T thyme
1½ tsp cayenne pepper
1½ tsp black pepper
1½ tsp sage
1½ tsp cumin
¾ tsp nutmeg
¾ tsp cinnamon

Jerk Chicken

5 T jerk seasoning (p.71)
2 cloves garlic, minced
1/4 cup olive oil
1/4 cup soy sauce
1/4 cup white vinegar
1/2 cup orange juice
1 lime, juiced
1 jalapeno, seeded and diced
3 green onions, chopped
1 red onion, chopped
4 chicken breasts

1. Combine ingredients in a large bowl. Cover with plastic wrap and marinate in refrigerator for several hours or overnight.
2. Cook on a hot grill until chicken is done, about six minutes per side. (Alternately, this dish could be prepared in a skillet on the stove.)

Food Profile: Jerk Foods

Jerk foods are so named because they were originally "jerked" with a sharp object to tenderize the meat. This method was used by the native Jamaican peoples before they placed an animal in a deep pit lined with hot stones to roast for many hours. The same mixture of spices is still used today. Besides jerk chicken, you can also taste jerk pork, fish, beef, and even goat in Jamaica.

- The Arawaks, the native people of Jamaica, invented the hammock.
- Coffee from Jamaica's Blue Mountains is the most expensive coffee in the world.
- The ackee is a unique Jamaican fruit. If eaten before fully ripened, it is poisonous!

Rice and Beans

Coconut Milk is made from the pulp of Coconut. It is found in a can in the Asian Foods section of the grocery.

1½ cups coconut milk
3½ cups water
1 (16 oz) can kidney beans, drained
4 garlic cloves, chopped
3 green onions, chopped
2 sprigs fresh thyme, chopped
1 tsp salt
1 tsp pepper
1 jalapeno pepper, whole
2 cups long-grain rice

1. Bring coconut milk, water, beans, and garlic to a boil. Simmer for three minutes. Add onion, thyme, salt, and pepper. Simmer for three minutes.
2. Stir in jalapeno pepper and rice. Return a boil.
3. Boil until rice is soft and liquid is absorbed, about twenty minutes.

Make More Than Dinner!

Mexico occupies the southern half of North America. The food of Mexico is rich with spicy flavors and bright colors. The great taste and simple preparation of Mexican cuisine has made it popular all over the world. *Comida* is the Mexican word for lunch. In Mexico, most businesses close from two to four o'clock in the afternoon. Everyone goes home and eats *comida,* which is followed by a *siesta,* a short rest or nap.

Make A Piñata

A piñata is usually made of papier-mâché or clay in the shape of an animal. It is used at special Mexican celebrations, such as a birthday party or Christmas dinner. You can make your own version by decorating a brown paper bag. Fill your piñata with candy and small toys. Have an adult help you hang it from the ceiling or a tree branch. To break it open, take turns hitting it with a bat while blindfolded. When it breaks open, hurry and get as much candy as you can!

Salsa Roja (Red Salsa)

Salsas of all kinds are served with every meal in Mexico. They are used as more than just a dip for chips. They go in soups, salads, rice—just about anything!

4 large plum tomatoes, seeded and diced
1 onion, diced
1/4 cup fresh cilantro, chopped
1 garlic clove, crushed
1 small bell pepper, chopped
2 limes, juiced
1–3 jalapeno peppers, seeded and chopped
salt
pepper

1. Combine tomatoes, onion, cilantro, garlic, bell pepper, and lime juice. Add one or more jalapenos, depending on how hot you like your salsa. Season with salt and pepper to taste.

2. Chill and serve cold. If you prefer your salsa cooked, simmer over low heat in a half cup of chicken stock for about ten minutes or until vegetables are soft. Drain and chill before serving.

Enchiladas

To make these enchiladas a complete meal, add cooked shredded chicken or ground beef.

vegetable oil
8 corn tortillas

1 jar (17.25 oz) mild enchilada sauce
3 cups mozzarella cheese, shredded

1. Preheat oven to 400°F. Heat a thin layer of vegetable oil over low heat on stove. Using a pair of tongs, dip each tortilla in the oil for about three seconds on each side. (This softens the tortilla and makes it easier to fold.) Drain on paper towels.
2. Spread a baking dish with a thin layer of the enchilada sauce, then poor remaining sauce into a large bowl. Dip a tortilla in the sauce, then place approximately a third cup of cheese down the middle (more or less depending on how you like it). Fold over and place in baking dish, seam side down. Repeat with remaining tortillas.
3. Pour any leftover sauce over the enchiladas, and sprinkle with any remaining cheese. Bake in oven for twelve to fifteen minutes, or until cheese is melted.

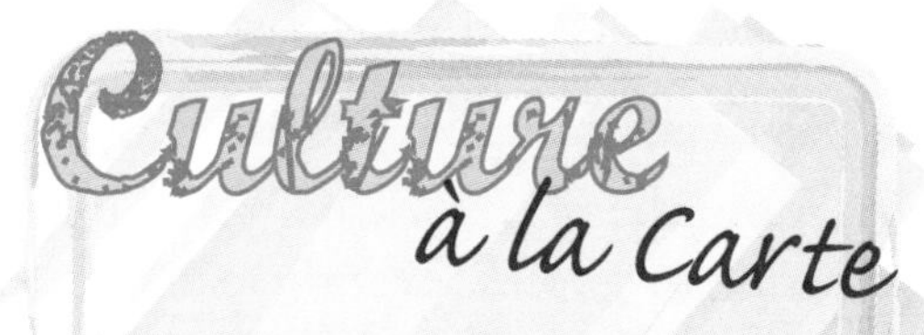

- Grasshoppers were eaten by the native Mexicans, and still are in some parts of the country.
- When going to dinner in Mexico, it is considered rude to be on time. In fact, it is standard practice to be two to three hours late. This gives the term "fashionably late" a whole new meaning!"
- In ancient Mexico, cocoa beans were used as currency. Only the very wealthy could afford to drink hot chocolate, since they were essentially drinking money!

Food Profile: Corn

Corn is the staple food of Mexico. It is used in many dishes, especially breads, and eaten in some form with every meal. In fact, the average Mexican eats four hundred pounds of corn a year!

An ear of corn always has an even number or rows, usually sixteen. It also contains an average of eight hundred kernels, with one corn silk for each kernel. The next time you eat corn on the cob, try to count the kernels to see how close it comes to the average!

Rice

2 T vegetable oil
1 garlic clove, minced
1 small onion, chopped
1½ cups long grain rice
2 cups chicken stock
1 cup canned corn, drained
1 cup tomato sauce
2 tomatoes, seeded and diced
salt
pepper

1. Heat oil in a medium saucepan. Saute the garlic and onion in oil until softened.
2. Stir in the rice, stock, corn, and tomato sauce. Bring to a boil. Cover the pan and reduce heat to low. Simmer for fifteen minutes, or until most of the liquid is absorbed.
3. Add tomatoes and continue cooking until all of the water is absorbed. Season with salt and pepper to taste. Serve.

Make More Than Dinner!

Many food scholars believe that the United States does not have a distinct food culture. It is a "melting pot" of many different cultures. Most of the popular food, like pizza or tacos, originated from other countries. If you want a bigger meal, try selecting some recipes from other countries for this one!

The History of Dinner

Here is a fun research project. Have each child select their favorite recipe. Using the internet and the library, have them research it. Some good questions to answer are:

- Who invented the dish?
- Where did it originate?
- How did it end up in this country?
- How has it changed over the years?
- In what other countries is it popular?
- What are some different ways it is prepared?
- What other recipes are based on this one?

Fried Chicken

1 (2–4 lb) chicken, cut in pieces
1 cup flour
1 tsp paprika
salt
pepper
vegetable oil

1. Fill a deep skillet with a half-inch layer of vegetable oil. Heat to medium.
2. Stir together flour and paprika. Add salt and pepper to taste. Roll chicken in flour mixture.
3. Gently add chicken to hot oil. Cover and cook until golden brown, turning once. Drain on paper towels. Serve.

Corn on the Cob

4 ears corn, husked
½ cup butter
salt
pepper

1. Preheat oven to 400°F. Place one ear of corn on a sheet of aluminum foil. Top with two tablespoons of butter, and sprinkle with salt and pepper. Wrap corn up tightly in aluminum foil. Repeat with remaining ears. Place on a cookie sheet or in a baking dish.
2. Bake for twenty to thirty minutes, turning corn with an oven mitt halfway through.

- The first printed mention of brownies was in a Sears & Roebuck catalog in 1897.
- Americans love their Italian food. On average, Americans eat forty-six slices of pizza per person per year. Americans purchase between one and a half to two million pounds of pasta every year.
- McDonald's® is the world's leading purchaser of beef.

Brownies

1 cup unsweetened cocoa powder
¼ tsp salt
1 cup flour
2 cups sugar
2 eggs
½ cup butter, melted
2 tsp vanilla

1. Preheat oven to 300°F. In a large mixing bowl, stir together ingredients into a thick batter.
2. Spread ingredients into a greased 9×13 baking dish. Bake for thirty minutes or until a toothpick inserted in the middle comes out nearly clean. Serve warm.

Make More Than Dinner!

South America

The country of Argentina is one of the world's leading producers of beef. The citizens are also the world's leading consumers of beef, eating a whopping 140 pounds per person per year. Therefore, many dishes in Argentinean cuisine contain beef as the main ingredient. Vegetarians would be quite out of place in this meat-loving country!

Carbonada Criolla

This stew features a unique combination of beef, vegetables, and fruit.

2 T olive oil
1 lb beef stew meat, cubed
2 tomatoes, chopped
1 green pepper, chopped
1 onion, chopped
1 clove garlic, minced
1 bay leaf
½ tsp oregano
1½ cups beef stock
2 potatoes, diced
1 sweet potato, diced
1 cup corn
1 zucchini, diced
1 peach, chopped
1 pear, chopped
salt
pepper
fresh cilantro, chopped

1. Heat oil in a stock pot. Brown beef; remove from pot and set aside. Reserve 2 tablespoons of drippings in pot; discard remainder.
2. Cook tomatoes, pepper, onion, and garlic in drippings until all are soft. Return beef to pot. Add bay leaf, oregano, and beef stock. Bring to a boil. Add potatoes and sweet potatoes; cover and simmer for fifteen minutes.
3. Add zucchini and corn. Simmer fifteen more minutes, or until vegetables begin to soften. Add peach and pear. Simmer five more minutes. Add salt and pepper to taste. Garnish with cilantro. Serve.

Zapallitos Rellenos (Stuffed Zucchini)

2 zucchini
2 T olive oil
1 onion, chopped
¾ cups bread crumbs
½ cup milk
1 egg, beaten
½ cup Monterey Jack cheese, shredded
salt
pepper
2 T melted butter

1. Preheat oven to 375°F. Bake zucchini for thirty minutes. Remove from oven and cool.
2. Saute onion in olive oil over medium heat until golden brown. In a large bowl, combine onion with bread crumbs, milk, egg, and salt and pepper to taste.
3. Slice the zucchini in half and scoop out the pulp. Add pulp to onion mixture; stir. Stuff the zucchini shells with mixture. Brush with melted butter and top with cheese. Bake for twenty five minutes. Serve.

- Potato dumplings were once served as the last meal of the month because that is all that a family could afford. More recently, it has become common practice to serve the dumplings with a peso under each plate as good luck, and to show that there is still some money left to be spent.
- Mate is the national drink of Argentina. It is an herb tea which is drank from a dried gourd with a metal straw.
- Stuffed zucchini flowers are considered a delicacy in some parts of the world.

Food Profile: Zucchini

The zucchini, a type of squash, was first imported into Argentina by Italian immigrants. It has since become popular all over the country. The best zucchini are firm with shiny, unblemished skin. The smaller a zucchini, the more flavor it will have. The best way to store a zucchini is in the refrigerator.

Budin (Sweet Bread)

This delicious bread tastes similar to pound cake.

2 cups flour
2 tsp baking powder
½ tsp salt
1 cup sugar
1 cup cream
2 eggs
2 tsp vanilla

1. Preheat oven to 350°F. Combine dry ingredients in a bowl. Stir in cream, eggs, and vanilla.
2. Pour into a greased baking dish. Bake for forty to forty-five minutes or until a toothpick inserted in the middle comes out clean.

Make More Than Dinner!

Brazil's cuisine is a reflection of its racially diverse culture. Alongside the native Brazilians, Portuguese settlers and their African slaves began establishing colonies in country around 1530. This mixed cuisine is complemented by the huge range of fruits, vegetables, and other food resources produced in South America's largest country.

Feijoada (Meat Stew)

2 strips bacon, chopped
1 onion, chopped
1 garlic clove, chopped
1 lb smoked sausage, chopped
1 lb beef stewing meat, chopped
1 can (14 oz) stewed tomatoes
1 T mustard
1 cup water
1 bay leaf
2 cups canned black beans
salt
pepper
2 oranges, peeled and sliced

1. In a large soup pot, cook bacon for three minutes. Add onion and garlic; saute until onion is soft. Add sausage and beef; cook until browned.
2. Add the tomatoes (undrained), mustard, water, and bay leaf. Bring to a boil. Reduce heat and simmer, covered, for an hour.
3. Add black beans and salt and pepper to taste. Simmer another ten minutes. Serve with sliced oranges on top.

Food Profile: Oranges

Brazil grows more oranges than any other country in the world, with navel oranges being the most popular for eating. To select a good orange, pick one that is heavy with no soft spots. Avoid oranges that are bruised or brown. You can store oranges at room temperature or they will keep for two or three weeks in the refrigerator.

Couve (Collard Greens)

1 bunch (about 1 lb) collard greens
1 T olive oil
1 T butter
1 shallot, minced
1 garlic clove, minced
salt
pepper

1. To prepare the collard greens, cut out the center stem of each leaf. Then roll the leaves and cut crosswise into thin strips.
2. Heat the olive oil and butter in a medium skillet. Add shallot and garlic; saute until soft. Add greens; saute until greens reach desired degree of doneness. Add salt and pepper to taste. Serve hot.

Ambrosia

6 eggs, beaten
½ cup orange juice
1 cup sugar

1. Preheat oven to 300°F. Combine ingredients in a bowl; pour into a baking dish.
2. Bake until top begins to brown, about an hour. Chill and serve cold.

Culture à la Carte

- Brazil produces about twenty percent of the world's coffee. A common Brazilian breakfast is a cup of coffee and a piece of bread.
- Brazilians eat a wide variety of toppings on their hot dogs. Some examples include mashed potatoes, corn, peas, and even quail eggs.
- Because orange blossoms are a symbol of good fortune, they are often used in flower arrangements for weddings.

Make More Than Dinner!

The fame of Peru's cuisine is slowly spreading all over the world. Some people believe that Peruvian restaurants will soon be as popular as Chinese, Mexican, or Italian restaurants. For now though, taste some Peru at home.

Papas a la Huancaina (Potatoes with Cheese)

4 potatoes, peeled and cubed
water
¾ cups heavy cream
¼ tsp turmeric
1½ cups Monterey Jack cheese

1. Place the potatoes in a saucepan and cover with water. Boil until tender. Drain and set aside.
2. In a small saucepan, heat cream over low heat. (Do not bring to a boil.) Stir in cheese and turmeric. Continue to stir until cheese is melted. Add potatoes, cooking until potatoes are heated through. Serve warm or cold.

Alfajores (Caramel-filled Cookies)

2 cups cornstarch (Yes 2 cups, really!)
1 cup flour
1 cup sugar
½ tsp baking powder
¾ cups butter, room temperature
2 eggs
1 tsp vanilla
3 T milk
1 can (13.4 oz) Dulce de Leche
Powdered sugar

1. Preheat oven to 300°F. Combine dry ingredients in a large bowl. Cut in butter and stir until the mixture resembles course crumbs. Add eggs, vanilla, and milk. Knead until smooth. Let dough rest for twenty minutes.
2. Roll dough out at about ¼ inch thickness. Cut out cookies with a cookie cutter. Bake for twenty minutes or until cookies begin to brown. Remove from oven and cool.
3. Spread dulce de leche on one side of the cookie and top with another cookie. Roll cookie sandwich in powdered sugar. Repeat with remaining cookies. Serve.

Dulce de Leche

1 can sweetened condensed milk

1. Remove the label from a can of sweetened condensed milk. Pierce the top, using a can opener, with two holes.
2. Place in a pot, pierced end up, and fill pot with water about a quarter-inch from the top of the can.
3. Bring to a boil. Reduce heat and simmer, uncovered, for three hours. You may need to add more water as the water evaporates.
4. Remove from water and cool.

Culture à la Carte

- Guinea pig is a common dinner in Peru.
- Lima beans are named for Lima, the capital city of Peru.
- Llamas are raised not only for their wool, but for their milk as well.

Food Profile: Dulce de Leche

Dulce de Leche, which translates to "milk jam," is a caramel dessert spread that is popular all over Latin America. You can purchase it in the Latin foods section at your local grocery. Legend has it that a woman was preparing a drink made with milk and sugar and forgetfully left it too long on the stove. The result was the tasty brown jam, Dulce de Leche.

Arroz con Pollo (Rice with Chicken)

3 T vegetable oil
4 boneless, skinless chicken breasts, sliced
1 onion, chopped
1 red pepper, seeded and chopped
1 clove garlic, minced
4 cups chicken stock
2 cups long grain rice
1 jalapeno, seeded and chopped
1/4 cup cilantro, chopped
1/4 tsp cumin
1 cup canned or frozen peas
salt
pepper

1. In a medium stock pot, brown chicken in oil. Remove chicken from pan and set aside. In the same pot, saute onion, red pepper, and garlic until tender.

2. Return chicken to pot along with chicken stock, rice, jalapeno, cilantro, and cumin. Bring to a boil. Reduce heat and simmer until most of the liquid is absorbed. Add peas. Continue cooking until all the liquid is absorbed, stirring frequently. Add salt and pepper to taste. Serve.

Make More Than Dinner!

Venezuela was named by Spanish explorers. Its name means "Little Venice," because the native peoples had built homes on the water which reminded the explorers of Venice, Italy. The architecture may have been similar, but the food was quite different! Enjoy this sample of Venezuela!

Cachapas (Corn Pancakes)

4 cups canned corn
1 tsp salt
¼ cup milk
½ cup sugar
1 egg
corn meal
vegetable oil
Monterey Jack cheese

1. Combine corn, salt, milk, sugar, and egg in a blender. Blend well. The mix should be the consistency of pancake batter. If it needs to be thicker, add some corn meal. To thin the batter, add more milk.

2. Heat a thin layer of vegetable oil in a skillet. Pour batter into skillet in small circles (just like pancakes). Sprinkle with cheese. When mixture begins to bubble (after about two minutes), flip with a spatula. Cook for two more minutes. Remove from skillet.

3. Repeat step two with remaining batter. Serve warm.

Pabellon (Pulled Beef)

5 T olive oil, divided
1½ lb rump roast
water
1 onion, chopped
1 garlic clove, chopped
1 red bell pepper, chopped
1 can (14 oz) diced tomatoes
½ tsp cumin
2 T fresh cilantro, chopped
1 tsp salt

1. Heat three tablespoons of the oil over medium heat in a medium saucepan. Brown beef on all sides in oil. Add enough water to cover beef. Bring to a boil. Cover, reduce heat to low, and simmer until meat is tender, about two hours.
2. In a separate skillet, heat remaining olive oil. Add onion, garlic, red pepper, salt, cumin, and cilantro. Saute until vegetables are tender. Add tomatoes with juice, and simmer, uncovered, until tomato juice has evaporated (about thirty minutes).
3. Remove beef from pot and set aside until cool enough to touch. Shred beef and add to skillet with vegetables. Stir until beef is heated. Serve warm with cooked black beans and white rice, if desired.

- Spanish conquistadors extracted a liquid from avocado seeds that they used as ink – the writing can still be seen today!
- It is an old Venezuelan tradition to eat lentils on New Year's Eve to bring wealth for the coming year.
- The avocado is sometimes called the alligator pear because its rough skin is like that of an alligator!

Food Profile: Avocado

The avocado is a fixture of South American cuisine. It is a very healthful fruit, containing more potassium than a banana. Choose an avocado that is heavy and free of any scrapes or cuts on the skin. A ripe avocado will be slightly soft to the touch. An overripe avocado, which is still useful for mashing, is extremely soft. Avocados can be stored at room temperature, but will last longer in the refrigerator. To prevent it from turning brown after cutting, rub the surface with some lemon or lime juice.

Guasacaca

This salsa, pronounced wah-sah-kaka, is similiar to guacamole. Serve with tortilla chips for dipping.

2 avocados, peeled and diced
2 tomatoes, seeded and diced
1 onion, diced
1 jalapeno, seeded and diced
1 T fresh parsley, chopped
1 T fresh cilantro, chopped
¼ cup red wine vinegar
1 tsp lemon juice
1 T salt
¼ tsp pepper

1. Combine all ingredients in a bowl. For extra hotness, add two teaspoons of hot sauce.
2. Chill in refrigerator. Serve cold.

Make More Than Dinner!

Oceania

Native Australians, Aborigines, were largely isolated from the rest of the world until the arrival of the British in 1770. While the Aborigines mainly lived off of the land, eating plants, animals, and insects, the new settlers longed for a taste of home. Thus, for many years, Australian food was imported from Britain. Fifty years ago, a typical Australian menu would look much like a British menu, but, now, times have changed. While Australian cuisine still has English influences at its foundations, it now draws heavy influences from neighboring Asia, as well as from the food eaten by natives.

Have an Aussie Barbecue!

The Australian word "barbie" is slang for barbecue. You can host your own "barbie" the next time you have a warm, sunny day. Heat up the grill, invite plenty of friends, and start cooking! Aussies are known for being laid-back, so be sure not to stress over this meal. If you don't have a grill at home, you might be able to use one at a local park. Barbecuing at the park is a favorite weekend activity in Australia.

Lamb Chops

If you cannot locate currant jelly, use grape jelly instead.

2 T currant jelly
2 T ketchup
2 T soy sauce
2 T brown sugar
1 T ground mustard
2 tsp Worcestershire sauce
4 lamb loin chops
8 slices pineapple

1. Preheat grill. Stir together jelly, ketchup, soy sauce, brown sugar, mustard, and Worcestershire sauce. Add lamb chops, cover, and refrigerate for at least fifteen minutes.

2. Place lamb chops and pineapple on grill. Discard leftover marinade. Grill pineapple for seven minutes, turning once. Grill lamb until it is cooked to your preference, about nine minutes for rare, thirteen minutes for medium, or eighteen minutes for well done.

Shrimp

Seafood is abundant along the coastlines of Australia, making it readily available for meals. Buying the shrimp already peeled, cleaned, and cooked makes preparing this dish easy!

½ cup butter, melted
¼ cup olive oil
¼ cup fresh herbs, minced (parsley, thyme, and cilantro)
juice from 1 lemon
3 garlic cloves, crushed
1 T shallot, minced
salt and pepper
1 lb peeled and cooked shrimp

1. Combine all ingredients in a plastic container and give them a good shake! Marinate for four to six hours.
2. Heat up the grill and thread shrimp onto barbecue skewers. (If you use wooden skewers, it is always a good idea to soak them in water first so they do not catch on fire.)
3. Cook shrimp until it is lightly browned on all sides. Serve on a platter lined with spinach and lemon wedges.

Culture à la Carte

- The Granny Smith apple was named for the Australian woman who first cultivated it, Maria Ann Smith.
- Macadamian Nuts are native to Australia, and were named for John Macadam, the man who first encouraged commercial cultivation of the nut.
- Kangaroo was once a common meal in Australia! It is still eaten in some parts of the country.

Anzac Biscuits

Anzac stands for Australia and New Zealand Army Corps. Legend has it these cookies, chosen because they store well, were shipped to ANZAC soldiers during the first World War by their loved ones who remained at home.

1 cup quick cooking oats
3/4 cups coconut flakes
1 cup all-purpose flour
1 cup sugar
1/2 cup butter
1 T honey
3 T water
1 tsp baking soda

1. Preheat oven to 350°F. Combine oats, coconut, flour, and sugar in a bowl; set aside.
2. In a small skillet, heat butter, honey, and water to a low boil. Stir in baking soda. Empty skillet into dry ingredients. Stir well. Roll into balls and place on a cookie sheet covered with parchment paper.
3. Bake for fifteen to eighteeen minutes or until golden brown.

Say What!

English is Australia's official language, but Australians have quite a few words that are all their own!

a feed: a meal
biscuit: cookie
bloke: a male person
chook: chicken
cuppa: a cup of tea
sheila: a female person
snags: sausages
tucker: food

Make More Than Dinner!

New Zealand

The rolling green hills of New Zealand make it a great place for the raising of livestock. Anywhere on the island, the furthest you can be from the ocean is eighty miles, so seafood is also abundant. Because of their close proximity, much of New Zealand's history, as its cuisine, is shared with Australia. The creation of Pavlova, for example, is claimed by both countries!

Pumpkin Soup

2 T butter
1 onion, chopped
3 stalks celery, chopped
1 clove garlic, crushed
¼ cup flour
2 cups pumpkin, peeled and cubed
4 cups chicken stock
1 T fresh parsley, chopped
1 T fresh thyme, chopped
1 bay leaf, crushed
salt
pepper

1. Melt the butter over medium heat. Add onions, celery, and garlic; saute until vegetables begin to soften.
2. Add flour, pumpkin, chicken stock, parsley, thyme, and bay leaf. Bring to a boil, stirring until flour is dissolved.
3. Reduce heat to low, and simmer until vegetables are soft, about one hour. Add salt and pepper to taste. Serve.

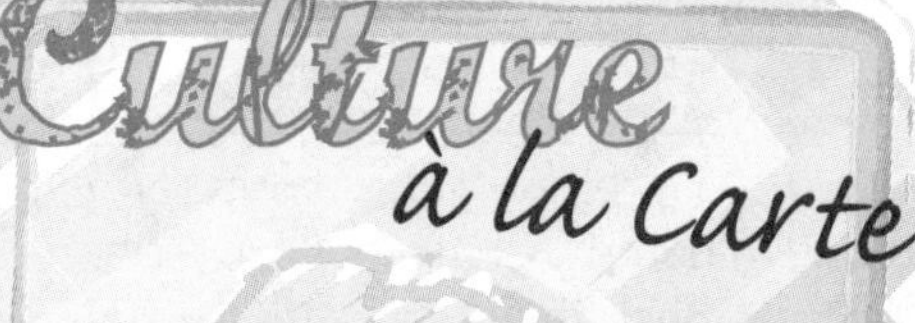

- New Zealand has a ten to one ratio of sheep to humans.
- The pumpkin is actually a fruit, not a vegetable.
- The world's largest pumpkin weighed in at 1,502 pounds.

Pavlova

This dessert was named for a Russian ballerina, Anna Pavlova, who visited New Zealand in the early 1900s. A chef created this dessert to be as delicate as the Russian ballerina herself.

3 egg whites, room temperature
1/8 tsp salt
1 tsp lemon juice
1 cup sugar
1 T cornstarch
whipped cream
2 kiwis, peeled and sliced
4 strawberries, sliced

1. Preheat oven to 250°F. Line a baking sheet with parchment paper. Beat the egg whites until they begin to foam, then add salt and lemon juice. Continue to beat until soft peaks form. Slowly add the sugar. Continue to beat until stiff, glossy peaks form. Gently fold in the cornstarch.
2. Using a spatula, place the beaten egg whites in a circle (like a thick pie) on the baking sheet. This is easier if you draw a circle on the parchment paper first to use as a guide. Bake in the oven for one hour. After baking is complete, turn off the oven and leave Pavlova in the oven to cool, for at least half an hour.
3. Gently slide Pavlova from the parchment paper onto a serving dish. Immediately before serving, top meringue with whipped cream, kiwis, and strawberries. Serve.

Food Profile: Kiwi

The Kiwi was originally exported to New Zealand from China under the name "Chinese Gooseberry." When New Zealand farmers decided to export their crop to the Western Hemisphere, they changed the name to kiwifruit, after their national bird, the Kiwi. (They feared that a name featuring the Chinese would be unpopular because this was during the height of the Cold War.) This sweet green-fleshed fruit has since become wildly popular all over the world. To select the best Kiwi, choose one that is slightly soft, but not mushy. A firm Kiwi still needs to ripen. The fastest way to do this is in a brown paper bag with an apple or pear for a day or two. (The gas released from the other fruits speeds up the ripening process.)

Damper Bread

This bread would traditionally be made in the coals of a hot fire when camping!

4 cups flour
2 T baking powder
2 tsp salt
2 T butter, room temperature
1 cup milk
½ cup water

1. Preheat oven to 400°F. Stir together flour, baking powder, and salt. Stir in butter until the mixture resembles course crumbs.
2. Stir in milk and water. Knead until smooth. Shape into a mounded loaf. Place on greased baking sheet. Bake for thirty to forty minutes, until bread is lightly browned and sounds hollow when tapped.

Make More Than Dinner!

My Food Journal

Today's Date: ______________________

I ate this meal at ______________________

This meal was cooked by ______________________

The dishes that made up this meal were:

____

____

____

Draw a picture or place a food passport stamp here.

Describe your first impression of the food. How did it smell? How did it look?

____

Were there any special table settings or decorations? Describe them. ______

____

How did the food taste? ______________________

____

Which dish did you like the best? The least? ______________________

____

How was this meal different or similar to what you normally eat? ______

____

Did this meal remind you of anything in particular? What? ______

____

If you helped prepare the meal, was it simple or difficult? ______

____

Would you like to have this meal again? ______________________

____

What would you do to improve this meal for next time? ______

____

Passport Activity

Cut or copy the passport and staple the pages together in order. As you complete each meal have students rate the food. Tape or glue the country seals in the country column and rate the food in the rating column.

fold here

Food PASSPORT

E PLURIBUS UNUM

United States of America

Staple pages together at fold line.

Country | Visas | Rating

fold here

Food PASSPORT

UNITED STATES OF AMERICA

TYPE
P

CODE
WORLD

PASSPORT #
210897142

LAST NAME

FIRST NAME/MIDDLE INITIAL

NATIONALITY

DATE OF BIRTH

PLACE OF BIRTH

GENDER

YOUR PHOTO HERE

P<EATYOURWAY<<AROUNDTHEWORLD<<<<<<<<<<<<<<<<<<<<<<<<<<<<<

21089142FOOD5701273F1405279<<<<<<<<<<<<<<<<<<<<<<<<<<08

Country Visas Rating

fold here

Country Visas Rating

Center page. Staple at markings in the fold.

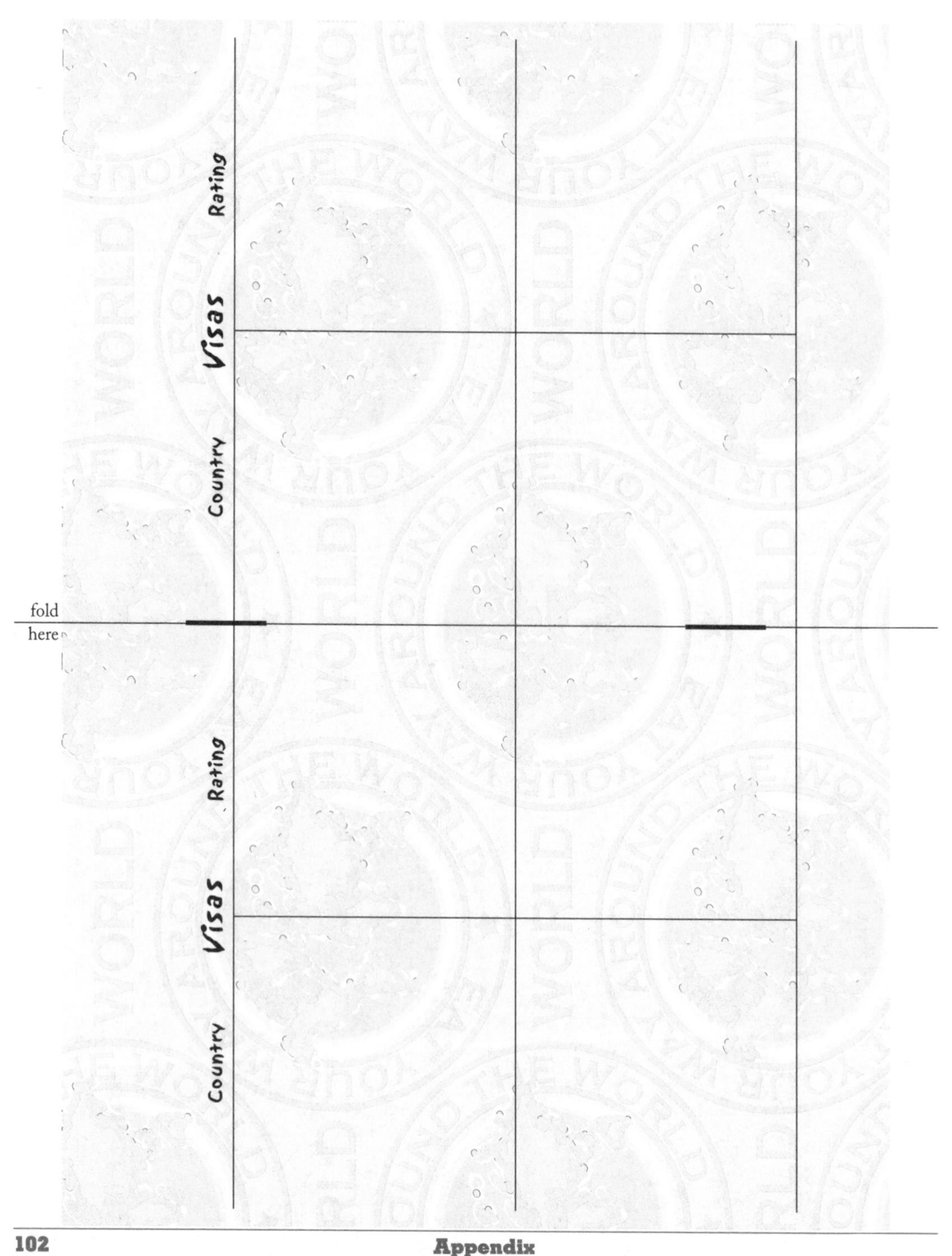

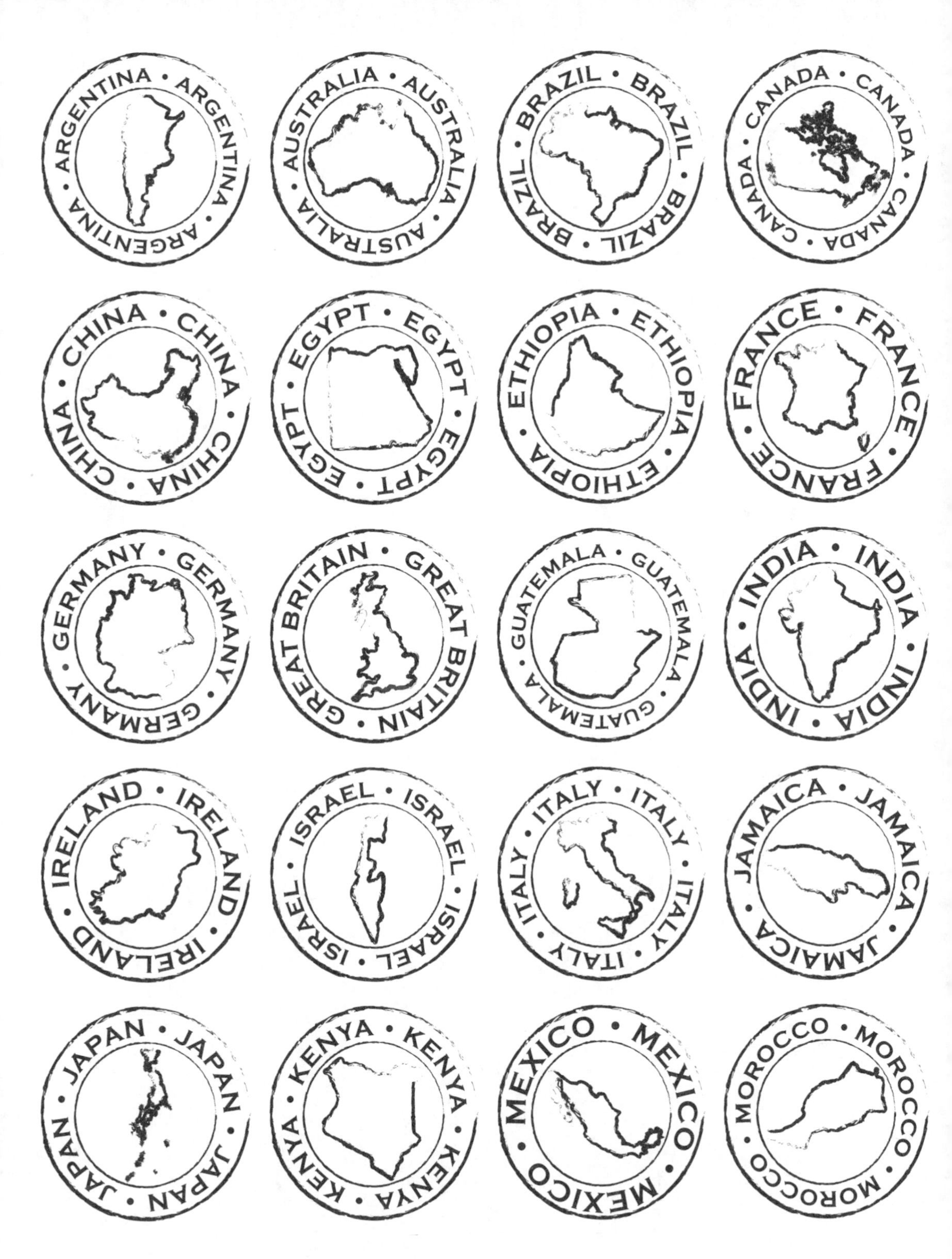

Hint: Print these on self adhesive paper to peel and stick on passport!

NETHERLANDS • NETHERLANDS • NETHERLANDS • NETHERLANDS
NEW ZEALAND • NEW ZEALAND • NEW ZEALAND • NEW ZEALAND
NIGERIA • NIGERIA • NIGERIA • NIGERIA
PERU • PERU • PERU • PERU
RUSSIA • RUSSIA • RUSSIA • RUSSIA
SOUTH AFRICA • SOUTH AFRICA • SOUTH AFRICA • SOUTH AFRICA
SOUTH KOREA • SOUTH KOREA • SOUTH KOREA • SOUTH KOREA
SPAIN • SPAIN • SPAIN • SPAIN
UNITED STATES • UNITED STATES • UNITED STATES • UNITED STATES
VENEZUELA • VENEZUELA • VENEZUELA • VENEZUELA
AVERAGE • AVERAGE • AVERAGE • AVERAGE
1
AVERAGE • AVERAGE • AVERAGE • AVERAGE
1
AVERAGE • AVERAGE • AVERAGE • AVERAGE
1
GOOD • GOOD • GOOD • GOOD
2
GOOD • GOOD • GOOD • GOOD
2
GOOD • GOOD • GOOD • GOOD
2
EXCELLENT • EXCELLENT • EXCELLENT • EXCELLENT
3
EXCELLENT • EXCELLENT • EXCELLENT • EXCELLENT
3
EXCELLENT • EXCELLENT • EXCELLENT • EXCELLENT
3
FAVORITE • FAVORITE • FAVORITE • FAVORITE

More Recipes

from the World Wide Web and beyond...

Africa

Egypt
- fooddownunder.com/cgi-bin/search.cgi?q=egyptian
- www.recipezaar.com/recipes/egyptian
- www.recipeatlas.com/egyptianrecipes/

Ethiopia
- fooddownunder.com/cgi-bin/search.cgi?q=ethiopian
- www.recipesource.com/ethnic/africa/ethiopian/
- www.recipezaar.com/r/235

Kenya
- kenya.rcbowen.com/wiki/index.php/Recipes
- nutford.kijabe.org/recipes.html
- www.blissites.com/kenya/culture/recipes.html

Morocco
- www.astray.com/recipes/?search=moroccan
- fooddownunder.com/cgi-bin/search.cgi?q=moroccan
- www.recipehound.com/Recipes/morocco.html

Nigeria
- www.motherlandnigeria.com/recipes.html
- www.recipezaar.com/recipes/nigerian
- www.onlinenigeria.com/recipes/recipes.asp

South Africa
- www.rainbownation.com/recipes/index.asp
- www.recipezaar.com/recipes/south-african
- fooddownunder.com/cgi-bin/search.cgi?q=south+africa

Asia

China
- www.recipesource.com/ethnic/asia/chinese
- www.chinesehomecooking.com
- fooddownunder.com/cgi-bin/search.cgi?q=Chinese

India
- www.indiaexpress.com/cooking/
- www.recipesindian.com
- www.cuisinecuisine.com/IndianCuisine.htm

Israel
- www.recipehound.com/Recipes/jewish.html
- www.jewishrecipes.org
- fooddownunder.com/cgi-bin/search.cgi?q=israel

Japan
- www.bento.com/tf-recp.html
- www.recipezaar.com/recipes.php?categ=cuisine%2Cjapanese
- www.recipehound.com/Recipes/japanese.html

South Korea
- fooddownunder.com/cgi-bin/search.cgi?q=korean
- www.asianonlinerecipes.com/online_recipes/korea/korea.php
- www.recipezaar.com/recipes.php?q=korean

Europe

France
- www.recipezaar.com/recipes/french
- frenchfood.about.com
- www.letscookfrench.com

Germany
- www.germany.info/relaunch/culture/life/recipe_archive.html
- www.elook.org/recipes/european/german1.html
- www.recipesource.com/ethnic/europe/german/

Great Britain
- www.bbc.co.uk/food/recipes/
- web.ukonline.co.uk/tuk/index.html
- www.greenchronicle.com/british_regional_recipes.htm

Ireland
- www.recipesource.com/ethnic/europe/irish/
- fooddownunder.com/cgi-bin/search.cgi?q=irish
- www.recipehound.com/Recipes/ireland.html

Italy
- www.completerecipes.com/italian1.htm
- www.gourmed.gr/italian-recipes/?gid=1&nodeid=12
- www.italianchef.com

Netherlands
- www.recipezaar.com/recipes/dutch
- fooddownunder.com/cgi-bin/search.cgi?q=dutch
- www.recipehound.com/Recipes/holland.html

Russia
- www.ruscuisine.com
- www.russian-crafts.com/russian-cuisine.html
- www.recipeland.com/category/view/?cid=246

Spain
- www.recipesource.com/ethnic/europe/spanish/
- fooddownunder.com/cgi-bin/search.cgi?=spanish
- www.gourmed.gr/recipes/spanish/?gid=1&nodeid=10

North America

Canada
- www.recipesource.com/ethnic/americas/canadian/
- www.recipezaar.com/recipes/canadian
- fooddownunder.com/cgi-bin/search.cgi?q=canadian

Guatemala
- www.recipezaar.com/recipes/guatemalan/
- fooddownunder.com/cgi-bin/search.cgi?q=guatemalan
- whats4eats.com/4rec_guatem.html

Jamaica
- fooddownunder.com/cgi-bin/search.cgi?q=jamaica
- www.jamaicans.com/cooking/
- www.caribbeanchoice.com/recipes/countryrecipe.asp?country=jamaica

Mexico
- fooddownunder.com/cgi-bin/search.cgi?q=mexican
- mexicanfood.about.com
- www.elook.org/recipes/latin/mexican1.html

United States
- allrecipes.com/Recipes/US-regional-and-ethnic/main.aspx
- www.recipezaar.com/browse/top/109
- fooddownunder.com/cgi-bin/search.cgi?q=usa
- To take a culinary tour of all fifty states, pick up a copy of *Eat Your Way Through the USA* by Loreé Pettit.

South America

Argentina
- fooddownunder.com/cgi-bin/search.cgi?q=Argentina&words=all
- www.popular-traditional-argentina-food.com
- www.recipezaar.com/recipes/argentinean

Brazil
- www.maria-brazil.org/brazilian_recipes.htm
- www.recipehound.com/Recipes/brazilian.html
- fooddownunder.org/cgij-bin/search.cgi?q=brazilian

Peru
- www.recipezaar.com/recipes/peruvian
- www.recipehound.com/Recipes/peru.html
- fooddownunder.com/cgi-bin/search.cgi?q=peru

Venezuela
- fooddownunder.com/cgi-bin/search.cgi?q=venezuela
- www.recipezaar.com/recipes/venezuelan
- www.recipehound.com/Recipes/venezuela.html

Oceania

Australia
- www.recipesource.com/ethnic/asia/australian/
- fooddownunder.com/cgi-bin/search.cgi?q=australian
- recipes.wuzzle.org/index.php/28

New Zealand
- www.recipezaar.com/recipes/new-zealand
- fooddownunder.com/cgi-bin/search.cgi?q=new+zealand
- www.elook.org/recipes/asian/new-zealand1.html

Index

Food Profiles

Other Fine Products Published by Geography Matters®

Eat Your Way Through the U.S.A.

The Adventures of Munford: Munford Meets Lewis & Clark

Geography Through Art

Cantering the Country

Galloping the Globe

Trail Guide to U.S. Geography

Trail Guide to World Geography

Trail Guide to Bible Geography

Laminated Outline Maps

Uncle Josh's Outline Map Book or CD-ROM

Mark-It Timeline of History

Historical & Bible Timeline Figures CD-ROM

Laminated USA Color Wall Maps

Laminated World Color Wall Maps

Contact us for our current catalog or log on to www.geomatters.com
Wholesale accounts and affiliates welcome.

(800) 426-4650 www.geomatters.com